connect, and enjoy nature than an indoor garden project.

PLANT CRAFT

PLANT CRAFT

30 PROJECTS THAT ADD NATURAL STYLE TO YOUR HOME

CAITLIN ATKINSON

TIMBER PRESS
Portland, Oregon

Published in 2016 by Timber Press, Inc.

The Haseltine Building
133 S.W. Second Avenue, Suite 450
Portland, Oregon 97204-3527
timberpress.com

Printed in China

Text design by Kristi Pfeffer
Cover design by Skye McNeill

Library of Congress Cataloging-in-Publication Data

Names: Atkinson, Caitlin, author.
Title: Plant craft : 30 projects that add natural style to your home /
   Caitlin Atkinson.
Description: Portland, Oregon: Timber Press, 2016. | Includes index.
Identifiers: LCCN 2015047576 | ISBN 9781604696493 (hardcover)
Subjects: LCSH: Indoor gardening. | Container gardening. | Nature craft.
Classification: LCC SB419 .A85 2016 | DDC 635.9/65—dc23 LC record
   available at https://lccn.loc.gov/2015047576

A catalog record for this book is also available from the British Library.

Contents

PREFACE

As a child I would help my mother pick flowers from our garden in summer and make bouquets in the cool of the early morning—my first exposure to the pleasures of working with plants. I loved summer and all the botanical wonder it brought. We lived on a farm, and when I wasn't in the garden I was often reading in the meadow or climbing trees. My life was spent outdoors, only coming in when too cold or wet. The land influenced me profoundly—seasons, light, weather, and topography lead me to new discoveries and creative endeavors. Throughout my life I've continued to feel the need to connect with the natural world. While living in San Francisco, in order to satisfy my desire to bring more green into my home, I began creating indoor garden projects. I have since moved and now have outdoor space, but I continue to bring the outdoors in.

I'm a photographer by trade, and my photography skills, along with my experience working as a stylist on photo shoots and a merchandiser at an urban garden shop, inform the aesthetics of the projects in these pages. The principles of balance in color choices, in texture combinations, and of creating a space for the viewer to enter a composition all draw on the same set of visual tools and apply to crafting and design as well as photography.

If you live in an urban environment these projects offer a way to connect with nature within the confines of a city. Not everyone can afford a rooftop garden or even a terrace, but everyone can make a little garden of their own indoors. If you have outdoor space, there is something invigorating about extending that green space indoors.

There is a project for everyone in this book. Create a colorful floral wall mural, an elegant table centerpiece, a serene underwater sculpture, or a whimsical mobile to suspend from the ceiling—each is a work of art inspired by the natural world.

Epiphytes are ideal plants for wall gardens. This one uses vanilla orchids, a personal favorite.

INTRODUCTION

Dried botanicals make a beautiful wall display.

As any gardener can tell you, working with plants and other natural materials forces you to accept the independent nature of the subject matter. An indoor garden can inspire a sense of wonder and anticipation, but also disappointment, and the unpredictability of working with natural materials can be a source of awe and frustration. An artist or crafter working with living things is forced to accept the impermanence of her creation and life itself—it is always a learning experience, and while mistakes can be made, fun can be had.

The projects in this book range from tabletop gardens to hanging sculptures to vertical wall gardens. A few are versatile and can be displayed by securing them to a wall or perching them on a bookshelf to lean against a wall. They vary in difficulty—a few, like the Water Sculpture Garden, merely call for assembling the materials to create the project while others, like the Bench Planter, require basic drilling know-how and comfort using a saw. Most can be made in an hour or two.

Given the right care, they all have the potential to grace your home for a long time. Some projects, such as the Miniature Flagstone Planting and the Saikei Tray Garden, are small living landscapes, which give you a chance to go beyond caring for a houseplant and fully engage your creative spirit as you select and arrange the materials and then tend to the plants.

There is no need to stop with the projects in these pages—use this book as a starting point. Seek inspiration for ideas in your daily life: from an art exhibit, a walk through a park, or a great book. Look to what is available in your local environment as well from afar when you're thinking about a new project. Exploring your surroundings closely is a way to develop a deeper connection to the place where you live. The need to connect with something beyond ourselves is necessary, the need to create, elemental. There is no better way to harness the desire to create, connect, and enjoy nature than an indoor garden project. Go get dirty.

Materials

PLANTS, CONTAINERS, AND DECORATIVE ELEMENTS

Look to your local garden and hardware stores for supplies such as plants and containers. Secondhand shops are also an excellent resource for containers, especially unusual ones. Keep in mind that containers need to have drainage holes, so if you're purchasing an unconventional container at a secondhand shop be sure it's something you can drill a drainage hole (or two) in.

If you're on the hunt for an unusual plant and don't see it at your nursery, don't forget that most nurseries and garden centers can usually special order a plant if they don't have what you're looking for in stock. You can often purchase samples or small amounts of flagstone, rocks, and gravel at your local landscape supply store. Online, Etsy is a great source for everything from handmade containers to wood.

DRIED BOTANICALS AND BOTANICAL EMULSIONS

Some of the projects in this book use dried botanicals. The key to featuring any dried botanical long-term is to display them in a place with low humidity and limit the amount of sunlight that reaches them. Preserved flowers can reabsorb water in the form of humidity and wilt. The more light in a room the faster the color in a dried botanical will fade, so it is best to display dried botanicals in a room that has low light and humidity.

The anthotype print project uses a photographic emulsion (the coating that creates the color of the print) made from botanical juice. As with dried botanicals, the more light in a room the faster the color in the print will fade, so it is best to display the anthotype prints in a room with little sunlight.

DRIFTWOOD

Prior to using driftwood you must cure it. The curing process leaches any excess tannins and salt. The best way to remove all toxins from driftwood is by boiling the wood for one to two hours. If you do not have a pot large enough to boil a piece of driftwood, you can soak the wood for two weeks, changing the water frequently. Driftwood from a lake is better than driftwood from the sea because of the amount of salt in wood from the sea. If you are using the driftwood submerged in water, such as in the Driftwood Water Garden, you may see some discoloration in the water after the curing process. The discoloration means that the tannins haven't been completely leached out (it can take weeks or months for the tannins to completely leach out). It won't harm the plants, but if you don't like it remove the wood from the vase and soak it some more until the water is clear.

FORAGED ELEMENTS

Driftwood, leaves, rocks, and small pieces of wood can also be foraged. A landscape can benefit from foraging if it's done with care and thought. For example, it is a great way to remove invasive species and help the habitat regenerate. It can also be devastating to the environment if done improperly, such as spreading the seeds of an invasive plant as you transport it. Native species or plants that you would like to retain in your landscape should be foraged selectively—never take all of the botanical materials from a single area. If you're foraging for branches do so when the trees are being pruned—it is wonderful to use parts of a tree that would otherwise be discarded. If in doubt don't forage; your local florist, flower market, and nursery are great sources for materials.

If you know someone who owns land ask them if you can forage on their property. Be aware that foraging on private property without the permission of the owner is illegal. You can often ask a property owner for permission to forage, but do not forage without permission. Rules vary from place to place, but foraging is often strictly limited or barred on most public lands. Consult your local park or county regulations before foraging on public land.

The Tillandsia Nest project uses foraged materials. Be sure to forage with care.

Plants

EPIPHYTES

I use epiphytic plants in many of the projects. Epiphytes are plants that put out roots to cling to trees, but they are not parasites—they don't take anything from the trees; they only use the tree, or host, as support. Many orchids, tillandsias, bromeliads, cacti, and ferns are epiphytes. They have adapted to obtain water and nutrients from the air, allowing them to flourish without being planted in soil. I love using them for indoor garden projects because they can be mounted or hung, which gives me more options to use them creatively.

AQUATIC PLANTS

Aquatic plants are grouped into three categories: emergent plants, submergent plants, and floaters. Emergent plants have foliage that emerges out of the water, so only their roots are anchored in the

soil. Submergent plants are also rooted in the soil, but remain under the surface of the water. Floaters float on the surface of water. When you're selecting aquatic plants it is important to determine if they are native to a warm- or cool-water climate—you'll need to know what temperature range they thrive in. Consult a reference book or a reliable online source. The water projects in this book use aquatic plants with lower light needs. Keep in mind that without the filtration system that accompanies an aquarium you will need to change the water for these projects every week.

CACTI

All cacti are succulents, but not all succulents are cacti. Cacti have small, round, cushion-like structures called areoles from which spines, branches, hair, leaves, and flowers grow. Cacti range from the spiny desert-dwellers to epiphytic rain-forest plants. Their sculptural shapes are showcased in the Cactus Clay Garden project. They are low-maintenance and can tolerate a little neglect. However, it's easy to overwater cacti. The best way to tell if cacti and other succulents are getting enough water is to see if they are plump—if they look puckered, they are thirsty. Most cacti are native to hot and dry climates and need a sunny spot to thrive indoors.

BROMELIADS AND TILLANDSIAS

Bromeliads are mainly native to South America, with the vast majority hailing from Brazil. The plants range from teeny to giant, with characteristics ranging from soft and dangly to prickly and structural. They can be found in dry deserts and moist rain forests. There are terrestrial species that grow in the ground; saxicolous species that grow on rocks (on either rocky outcroppings or in cracks); and epiphytic species that are found growing in trees or other plants. The epiphytic variety is great for use in mounting projects. The most well-known bromeliad is the pineapple. Tillandsias, Spanish moss, aechmea, billbergias, neoregelias, and guzmania are also bromeliads.

Many bromeliad species have a tank, or cup, created by the close overlapping of their central leaves. These tanks store water and collect nutrients (from leaf litter, forest debris, and insects). All bromeliads have trichomes, or tiny scales, along their leaves that function as an absorption system. The trichomes sometimes form patterns or bands on the leaves that add to the beauty of the bromeliad. Many bromeliads have long-lasting blooms, but once a bromeliad has bloomed the plant begins to die. The mother plant will produce

Many bromeliads have bold-colored foliage.
LEFT: *Rhipsalis*, an epiphytic cacti, mounted on a branch.

pups, or small plantlets, that will use the mother for nutrients until they produce their own roots.

Tillandsias, often called air plants because they do not need soil to live, are a type of bromeliad. You'll find them in the Tillandsia Nest and the Tillandsia Wall Hanging projects.

BONSAI

Bonsai simply means tray planting. The art form of tray gardening, known as Penjing, originated in China. Bonsai, along with saikei, *hòn non bộ*, and kokedama, stem from the original idea of creating a tray landscape. Some forms of tray landscapes emphasize the character of the individual tree (bonsai), while others evoke a miniature natural landscape (saikei). Originally bonsai was an outdoor practice. Moving it indoors meant changing the materials to trees and plants that would flourish indoors. Common houseplants like a jade plant or weeping fig can be trained as bonsai forms. Careful pruning of branches and roots will allow you to keep the plants in small trays. Bonsai and saikei tray gardens require more careful and frequent watering. A few of the tray garden projects use succulents in place of more traditional trees and moss; these plants have shallow root structures, so watering them is not quite as challenging.

FERNS

Ferns provide a wealth of texture, brightness, and form as well as a serene, lush look to a project. Give them enough light, moisture, and humidity and they will thrive.

MOSS

Moss is a beautiful way to add a luscious green texture to an indoor garden. Cushion, haircap, and rock cap moss can be used in terrariums and tray gardens. Sheet moss is used in the Living Wreath and Three-Fern Kokedama projects. Moss lacks a vascular system, so it absorbs water and nutrients mainly through its leaves. Since moss obtains its nutrients from air it requires adequate moisture, a firm soil bed, and sufficient light.

ORCHIDS

Orchids are exotic, flowering plants that I find hard to resist. They are an amazingly diverse group, and many have traits that make them appealing for an indoor garden project. The epiphytic miniatures are wonderful to mount. Often the flowers are the most prized feature, but I recommend looking at the foliage as well—it can add interest to an indoor garden all year long. They also have very specific needs, so finding the right ones for your climate is essential for success. With a little extra care and informed choices you can create a magical orchid display. Orchids that come from the equator do not tolerate much variation in temperature. If you are a beginner or don't live in an environment with a stable temperature, try to stay away from these orchids and instead pick plants that can handle a broader temperature range.

Mounted orchids require extra attention and water.

RIGHT: This Wardian case terrarium has a front roof hinged panel that allows for proper ventilation.

SUCCULENTS

It is a misconception that all succulents make great houseplants. Most rosette-shape succulents will not survive long-term indoors, including the incredibly popular echeveria and aeonium. Opt instead for a succulent that does well in shade outdoors, such as senecio, gasteria, haworthia, or rhipsalis. If you have a very sunny home, euphorbia or cacti will do well. Indoor light is more diffuse than outdoor light, so place your succulents in a bright sunny spot so that they thrive long-term. If you want a temporary indoor garden, then you can use any succulent. Succulents that require more light than they are receiving indoors can last for months without any problems, but they will eventually start to look like they are stretching. They are just looking for light.

A Guide to Growing and Maintaining Indoor Plants

The key to successfully growing plants indoors is creating the ideal environment with the right combination of different elements. Understanding where the plant is native can help you understand its ideal environment—check the plant's tag or label for information on its native habitat and care.

LIGHT

The optimum levels of light will ensure healthy, long-lived indoor plants. There are three categories of light needs: shaded, bright, and full sun. Most indoor environments will be shaded or at most bright, unless there is a south-facing window. Plants that need bright light can handle a little direct sun. Shaded does not mean no light—you still need to provide the plant with bright but indirect light. You can add growing lights to help your plants receive enough light, but be sure to pay attention to the humidity as growing lights decrease the amount of moisture in the air. The terms bright indirect, direct, or full sun are self-explanatory, but if you want to be exact you can use a light meter to determine the exact amount of light your home receives. Light is measured in foot-candles, which are equivalent to lumens per square foot (a lumen is a measurement of how much visible light is emitted from a light source).

The definition of high or full sun is 150–1,000 foot-candles (fc); medium or bright indirect light is 75–150 fc; and low or shaded light is 25–75 fc.

Light meters are available for measuring light intensities in indoor environments. Some may be purchased at relatively low cost from garden centers or online. Their readings of low, medium, and high can give you a rough idea of what type of light you have and can eliminate much of the guesswork in selecting plants. You can also easily determine more precisely how much light you have with a manual camera. The light will vary from morning until night and throughout the year, so take readings in morning, noon, and late afternoon to determine the average intensity throughout the day. Also consider the changes in the amount of daylight throughout the year based on the arc of the sun in the sky and the position of the sunrise and sunset on the horizon, and the length of day.

You can use a camera's light meter with the following conversions to foot-candles: set the ASA/ISO to 100 and the f/stop to 16. Place a sheet of white paper on the surface where the plant will be displayed and aim the camera at it from a high angle. The intensity of full sun in clean dry air is about 10,000

foot-candles, under which conditions your camera will indicate an exposure time of $\frac{1}{500}$ second.

$\frac{1}{500}$ second = 10,000 foot-candles

$\frac{1}{250}$ second = 5,000 foot-candles

$\frac{1}{125}$ second = 2,500 foot-candles

$\frac{1}{60}$ second = 1,250 foot-candles

In general, southeast or west-facing windows that receive direct sun will have high light. Areas that are four to eight feet from south-, west- and east-facing windows that do not receive direct sun will have medium light. Northern exposure or areas farther than eight feet out are considered low light.

It is important to remember that in winter the days are shorter and the arc of the sun is lower. Where the sun rises and sets shifts throughout the year, moving northward in summer and southward in winter. Often this means the growth period for indoor plants is during the longer days, when they receive more light. It also means that in winter, when the sun is lower, plants close to windows may receive more direct sun than during the summer. Other factors that may affect the amount of light a plant receives are roof lines, awnings, outdoor trees, buildings, reflected light from nearby buildings, paint color, and office lights.

Light is essential for any plant life.

You can supplement sunlight with indoor lighting. A plant grown completely with artificial light needs two bulbs set 12 inches above the plant for 12 to 16 hours. A combination of cool and warm fluorescent lights is the best and most economical option. Supplemental lighting can take the form of track lighting or another light fixture; the amount needed will vary depending on the amount of sunlight you are receiving and the output from your light fixture. Base the amount of light you give the plant on the needs of the individual plant.

TEMPERATURE

Most homes are heated and cooled to a comfortable temperature for the inhabitants, usually between 60°F to 80°F. Most plants that are grown as indoor houseplants have come from areas in the world where this is an agreeable temperature range. Some plants want to experience a nighttime drop in temperature, and many want a cooler winter rest period. Each plant will have specific needs, which should be described on its tag or label; if for some reason you cannot find information on the ideal

It is important to understand the quality, frequency, and duration of watering.

LEFT: If you have placed sun-loving plants in a windowsill, be sure to move them away from the window at night during cold winter months.

temperature range for a plant, find out where it is native for information on climate needs.

Within your home the temperature may vary from room to room. Use a thermometer to monitor the temperature throughout the day if you would like to get more precise data. The most detrimental changes in temperature are caused by drafts from a door or window in winter or burning heat from a glass window. You can use shades or curtains to provide relief or move the plants just out of range. Keep the plants away from air conditioners and fireplaces, furnaces, or heaters.

WATER
In addition to light, the correct amount of water at the right frequency is key to a plant's survival. The feel of the soil should be your main guide in watering indoor plants. When the top half-inch of the soil is dry it is time to water. When you water be sure the entire root ball is evenly moist and not just the surface of the soil. The plant needs moisture at its roots to survive. The best way to water the mounted orchids, moss-wrapped string gardens, kokedama, and living wreath in this book is to submerge the entire plant or structure in water. Once all the air bubbles have stopped coming to the surface the soil is fully saturated and you can remove them from the water.

Many indoor plants that are not given artificial light go into a resting stage during the short cool days of winter. During this season the frequency of watering should be reduced. Also be careful not to use water that is too cold—it could shock your plants. Leave water out overnight to have room temperature water and to allow chlorine to evaporate. Here are some tips that can be applied to most indoor plants:

》 In a warm, dry, sunny location plants need more frequent watering than they do in cool, low-light locations.

》 The same plant in summer will need more water than in winter.

》 A moss-wrapped plant, bonsai, mounted plant, or plant in a shallow planter will need more frequent watering than a traditional houseplant.

》 Plants with large or very thin leaves and those with fine surface roots usually require more frequent watering than succulent plants with fleshy leaves and stems that are able to store water internally.

》 Flowering plants and plants in a growing cycle (usually spring and summer) dry out more quickly than those in a resting stage (usually winter).

》 Thorough but less frequent water is better than frequent insufficient water.

》 If your plants have a top dressing of gravel or sand on them, they will need to be watered less often than those without.

》 If your tap water is hard water, use distilled water to water your plants, especially if you're caring for

bromeliads and carnivorous plants. Ideally, they'd prefer rainwater—if you can harvest rainwater, this would be the best thing for them.

» Rotate your plants after every watering to encourage even growth toward the light source.

HUMIDITY

Humidity plays an important role in determining which plants will do well in your environment. In dry air cacti and succulents will flourish, while the leaves of tropical plants may turn yellow or brown at the tips. Many houseplants are native to subtropical or tropical regions but can adapt to lower humidity levels—as low as 20 to 40 percent humidity. A cactus is at home in 5 to 15 percent humidity. Succulents can actually melt if exposed to an environment that is too humid. You can gauge the humidity with a hygrometer. Mist your plants at least once a day if they need humid conditions to survive. Air conditioners tend to dry out the air, and evaporative coolers can raise humidity. You can also invest in a dehumidifier or a room humidifier to decrease or increase a room's humidity levels. Some rooms, like kitchens and bathrooms, are naturally more humid.

SOIL

Different types of plants have different soil needs. A plant's soil preference is mostly determined by how moist it likes the soil to be, so how much water the soil retains and how quickly the soil drains are two considerations when you're pur-

chasing soil. Common ingredients in a soil mix are peat moss, perlite, bark, and vermiculite. Peat moss holds water, perlite helps circulate air, and bark and vermiculite hold water and nutrients and help create air channels in heavy soil. There are many mixes sold premixed to help you select the right one. For example, you can get a cactus and succulent mix, an African violet mix (which can also be used for ferns), a bonsai mix, or a general potting soil. When I first started looking at planting mediums I was quite confused by potting soil and planting mix. The difference between a potting soil and a planting mix is that potting soil is designed for growing plants in pots, so it has different water-retention rates than a planting mix, which is designed to be used in a garden bed, not a container. You should not use garden soil for indoor plants. Choosing the right soil for the plant you have selected is important for the health of the plant.

Over time the soil sinks due to decomposition and displacement. Often this can cause excessive water retention or decreased aeration, which can suffocate the roots. If a plant needs to be repotted, simply remove the plant from the pot and remove any excess soil from around the root ball, place a new layer of soil into the pot, place the root ball on top and fill the sides and top of the pot with new potting soil.

A daily misting will add humidity to a plant's environment.

RIGHT: Epiphytic plants that have been mounted, like this staghorn fern, do not require repotting.

AIR MOVEMENT

All plants grow better with air movement. A slight breeze helps them stay cool when it's hot and strengthens them. Placing a fan nearby is helpful, especially during the hotter months.

FERTILIZER

Fertilizer contains nitrogen (N), phosphorus (P), and potassium (K), which are usually indicated on the label in ratios, such as 5-10-5. The first number represents nitrogen, the second phosphorus, and the third potassium (N-P-K). Most plants grow vigorously with a balanced fertilizer. For a nonflowering plant you can use a fertilizer with a higher percentage of nitrogen.

There are specially formulated fertilizers for orchids, African violets, tillandsias, epiphytes, and cacti. Water-soluble fertilizers need to be measured and dissolved in water at each feeding. Slow-release fertilizers dissolve in the soil and are good for several months. Make notes on your calendar to keep track of when and how much fertilizer you gave a plant. Observe your plants to fine-tune your regimen. As a general rule, applications in spring and summer are recommended. During the winter rest period hold off on fertilizer. Plants that have just been transplanted or repotted will obtain sufficient nutrients from the fresh potting soil for at least four to eight weeks and do not require supplemental fertilizer during this time. It is always better to underfertilize than to overfertilize. I usually dilute water-soluble fertilizers and apply them only once or twice a year during a plant's active growing season (spring and summer).

GENERAL CARE AND MAINTENANCE

Dust settles quickly on leaves and is not only unattractive, but also interferes with the leaves' ability to function. Use a moist sponge or soft cloth to remove dirt and dust every couple of months. Remove yellow or dead foliage. If you are removing a brown leaf tip, use a sharp pair of scissors and trim down to the green, following the contour of the leaf for a more natural look.

CONTAINERS

When planning a project it is important to think about what type of plant will succeed in the selected container or planting technique. A plant will not thrive in a pot that is too large or too small. For most houseplants the diameter of the pot should be about one-third the height of the plant from the top of the foliage to the soil line. You can use plants with shallow roots, like cacti and succulents, in shallow containers. Moisture evaporates through the sides of terra-cotta or other untreated clay pottery, which provides aeration but also causes the plant to dry out faster. In most cases you do not need to place a layer of gravel at the bottom of a pot because it does not improve drainage—it just reduces soil volume. If you are using a container without drainage holes be careful not to overwater the plant. In general, it is better to use a pot with at least one drainage hole (several drainage holes would be ideal if the pot is large).

MOVING PLANTS OUTDOORS

If you have outdoor space, even a balcony or porch, you can move many of these projects outside during the warmer months. The plants will enjoy the fresh air and higher light, but you should transition them slowly to the outdoors starting with an hour or two each day. A spot in light shade outdoors

Keep your plants healthy for a long-lasting indoor garden.

is best for most indoor plants. There are a few plants like cacti, some bromeliads, and ponytail palms that enjoy full sun; otherwise avoid putting the plants in direct sun, especially during the hottest part of the year. The outdoor environment, with more light and more airflow, will mean that the plants will need more water.

PROPAGATION

If you are interested in propagating, many plants can be propagated from cuttings. There are propagation instructions for specific plants at the end of many of the projects.

PROBLEMS

If a plant is receiving proper light, water, airflow, humidity, and nutrients it will be vibrant and vigorous in its growth. Too much or too little water and light are the most common cause of problems. It is important to pay attention to how a plant is reacting and try to identify the reasons behind the symptoms. Droopy leaves can indicate that the plant needs water, but it could also mean the plant is getting too little water. Pests and diseases are more likely to attack plants that are stressed.

A neon pothos cutting, started in water, can continue to live with the roots growing in water.

IDENTIFYING PLANT PROBLEMS AND CAUSES

	Too much light	Not enough light	Underwatered	Overwatered	High temperature	Low temperature	Poor drainage	Lack of fertilizer	Excess fertilizer	Low humidity	Excess humidity
Wilted leaves	X		X	X	X		X		X	X	X
Yellow leaves	X	X		X	X		X		X	X	
Tips of leaves are brown			X	X			X	X	X	X	
Spots	X		X			X					
Bent and curled leaves						X				X	
Leaf drop			X	X			X		X	X	
Small new growth		X	X	X	X		X	X	X	X	
Leggy		X							X		
Soft and weak		X	X	X	X		X	X			
Fails to flower		X	X	X	X	X	X	X	X	X	
Less intense color		X		X			X	X			

PLANTS FOR YOUR HOME

NAME	COMMON NAME	NATIVE TO	FEATURES AND USES	CARE
Adiantum	maidenhair fern	Asia, South America, North America	Great for terrariums or humid spots; used in Three-Fern Kokedama.	Needs evenly moist soil and high humidity. Medium light; prefers temperatures above 70°F; don't let it drop below 60°F indoors. Don't place near cold drafts.
Aechmea fasciata	urn plant or silver vase	Brazil	Bromeliad; tropical appearance.	Keep tank full of water; don't overwater; mist the leaves occasionally during warm months. Medium light; 59°F–70°F. Feed once in spring and again in late summer.
Aegagropila linnaei	marimo, moss balls	Lakes in the Northern Hemisphere	Sculptural aquatic plant; used in the Water Sculpture Garden.	Roll the balls occasionally to clean and stimulate them.
Aeschynanthus	lipstick plant	Southeast Asia and the East Indies	Trailing epiphytes with showy flowers; great for the Hanging Rock Garden and the Lush Vertical Garden.	Consistent moisture without being overly wet. Medium light; prefers high humidity, 70°F–80°F ideal, keep above 50°F.
Aglaonema	Many varieties	Tropical and subtropical regions of Asia and New Guinea	Great foliage plant.	Water thoroughly in the summer and mist often to raise humidity (loves humidity). Medium to low light depending on variety. Temps above 65°F. Keep away from cold drafts.
Aloe vera	aloe vera	Mediterranean and North Africa	Succulent; medicinal uses; great as a potted plant on a shelf or windowsill.	High light, normal-to-low humidity; 70°F–80°F ideal, keep above 50°F. Use succulent-cactus soil mix.

IN PROJECTS AND BEYOND

NAME	COMMON NAME	NATIVE TO	FEATURES AND USES	CARE
Asparagus setaceus, *A. plumosus*, *A. retrofractus*	asparagus fern	Southern and eastern Africa	Graceful, soft foliage; great for the Bench Planter.	Soil should be kept lightly moist and allowed to just dry between waterings; mist occasionally. Medium light. Appreciates higher humidity; 70°F–75°F and 10°F cooler at night.
Aspidistra elatior	cast-iron plant	Eastern Himalayas, Taiwan, China, and Japan	Slow growing, great planted pot.	Tolerates neglect; keep evenly moist but not constantly wet; low light, as low as 10 foot-candles; 50°F–55°F at night and 70°F–75°F day, keep above 30°F. African violet soil mix.
Asplenium nidus	bird's nest fern		Epiphytic fern; could be used in a mounting project.	Moist soil; indirect light; high humidity; ideal temps 70°F–80°F—don't go below 55°F.
Beaucarnea	ponytail palm	Mexico	Distinctive trunk, structural; great as a specimen; use in bonsai and tray gardens.	Water thoroughly when soil dries out. High light, full sun. No lower than 45°F.
Billbergia	Many varieties	North and South America	Bromeliad; epiphyte; excellent for mounting.	Water by pouring distilled water into the cup formed at the base of the leaves. Some are cold-hardy to 26°F. Tolerant of temperature extremes.
Bromeliads	Many varieties	Mainly South America	Wonderful color; epiphytic varieties are great for mounting.	High to medium light—consult tags or labels for individual care needs.
Cacti	Many varieties		Sculptural; great colors and textures, used in the Cactus Clay Garden.	High to medium light—consult individual care needs.

PLANTS FOR YOUR HOME

NAME	COMMON NAME	NATIVE TO	FEATURES AND USES	CARE
Ceropegia woodii	string of hearts	South Africa, Swaziland, and Zimbabwe	Trailing succulent; ideal as a hanging plant or for a string garden.	Needs excellent drainage and should be watered only when dry. High light. Likes low humidity; ideal temperature 60°F–75°F.
Chlorophytum comosum 'Variegatum'	spider plant	South Pacific and South Africa	Use in a hanging planter or vertical garden.	Keep soil evenly moist. Medium light. Moderate humidity; 65°F–75°F; indoors don't let the temp fall below 50°F.
Cissus rhombifolia	grape ivy	South America	Wonderful glossy green foliage for the Lush Vertical Garden or the Single-Dowel Plant Hanger.	Keep evenly moist but not soggy. Low to medium light. Humidity 40%–60%; 65°F–80°F spring and summer; fall and winter 50°F–70°F.
Cissus rotundifolia	Arabian or Peruvian grape ivy	East Africa	Great for hanging; good for the Lush Vertical Garden or the Concrete Vine Planter.	Low water needs. Bright indirect to bright light.
Crassula argentea	jade plant	South Africa	Succulent; great for bonsai or tray garden.	Allow to dry out completely and then give it a good soak. High to medium light. Prefers 55°F at night and 75°F–80°F during the day; okay down to 40°F.
Croton	Many varieties	Southeast Asia	Bright colorful foliage; good as a stand-alone plant or in the Bench Planter.	Keep soil evenly moist; wilts easily if dry. High light needs to keep color. Prefers high humidity; will drop some leaves without it. Ideal temperature is 70°F during the day and 60°F at night.

IN PROJECTS AND BEYOND

NAME	COMMON NAME	NATIVE TO	FEATURES AND USES	CARE
Cryptanthus	Earth star	Brazil	Terrestrial bromeliad; should not be mounted. Great color. Works well in terrariums.	Moist soil. Medium light. Prefers high humidity. Ideal temperature range is 60°F–85°F. Use African violet mix.
Dieffenbachia	Several varieties; dumb cane	West Indies, tropical Americas	Works nicely for the Bench Planter.	Water often enough to keep the soil lightly moist but never soggy. Medium light. Likes temps between 65°F–80°F.
Dracaena	Many varieties	Mostly Africa	Tall structural shape; good stand-alone plant; would work well in Bench Planter.	Medium light, no direct sun. Prefers moderate to high humidity; 65°F–85°F, don't drop below 60°F.
Epipremnum aureum	pothos	Solomon Islands	Great climbing vine for the Concrete Vine Planter or lovely as a draping plant in the Lush Vertical Garden.	Tolerates underwatering better than overwatering. Medium light, but can tolerate lower light. Likes high humidity, but not necessary. Ideal temperature is 65°F–75°F; no lower than 50°F. Easy to grow; clip back to keep bushy.
Euphorbia californica		California	Used in the Lava Rock Bonsai.	Can tolerate dry soil. Cut back on watering in winter. Likes a sunny southern location.
Euphorbia decaryi		Madagascar	Interesting succulent with zigzag pattern on trunk. Great in a dish garden or bonsai pot; used in the Miniature Flagstone Planting.	High light needs. Caustic sap—care should be taken when handling. Use cactus potting soil mix.

PLANTS FOR YOUR HOME

NAME	COMMON NAME	NATIVE TO	FEATURES AND USES	CARE
Euphorbia tirucalli	pencil cactus	Madagascar	Succulent; good stand-alone plant or use in group planting like the Miniature Flagstone Planting.	Allow to dry between waterings. High light. Summer 65°F–70°F; cooler in winter. Caustic sap—care should be taken when handling. Use cactus potting soil mix. Can be pruned for shape.
Fatsia japonica	Japanese fatsia	Japan	Good as a single houseplant; could use in the Bench Planter.	Medium light; likes warmth and humidity.
Ficus benjamina, F. microcarpa, F. retusa	weeping fig, Cuban laurel, Chinese banyan, banyan fig	South and Southeast Asia and Australia	Good for bonsai; *Ficus benjamina* used in the Saikei Tray Garden.	Does not like overly wet roots; water when dry. Medium light. Keep out of drafts; likes a humid environment; prefers temperatures above 60°F.
Gasteria	ox tongue	South Africa	Great succulent for tray gardens.	Water evenly and thoroughly; allow to dry out before watering again. Medium-high light; avoid hot sun. Prefers a cooler winter, but will not tolerate temps lower than 40°F.
Gynura aurantiaca	purple passion plant or velvet plant	Indonesia	Lovely soft serrated green leaves; densely covered with purple hairs.	Keep the soil evenly moist spring through fall. Water less in winter. Do not get water drops on the leaves; it can damage them. Medium light. Moderate to high humidity. Likes 60°F–75°F. Use African violet soil mix.
Haworthia	Many varieties	South Africa	Small, compact succulent. Great for tray gardening; used in the Rock and Sand Landscape and Miniature Flagstone Planting.	Avoid overwatering. Medium to high light; keep away from hot sun. Prefers a cooler winter; will not tolerate temps lower than 40°F.

IN PROJECTS AND BEYOND

NAME	COMMON NAME	NATIVE TO	FEATURES AND USES	CARE
Hoya	wax plant, rope hoya, Hindu rope	Most native to Asia	A good vine for hanging. Would work in the Succulent String Garden or Lush Vertical Garden.	Water thoroughly and allow to dry between waterings. High light needs but can be conditioned to medium light needs. Prefers 50% humidity. Ideal temperatures 65°F–75°F. Can be pruned back to keep compact.
Humata tyermanii	rabbit's foot fern	Canary Islands	Epiphytic fern that can be mounted. Used in Living Wreath project; could also be mounted in a shadow box.	Low to moderate watering; allow to just dry out before watering. Can tolerate low light, but prefers bright indirect light. Prefers high humidity.
Maranta leuconeura var. *erythroneura*	red-veined prayer plant	Brazil	Good for hanging or in a vertical garden.	Evenly moist soil. Medium light. Prefers 50% humidity; ideal temperature range 65°F–80°F. Prefers peat-rich potting mix, like African violet mix.
Microsorum diversifolium	kangaroo paw fern	Australia	Suitable for the Lush Vertical Garden.	Prefers even moisture and bright indirect light.
Microsorum pteropus	Java fern	Southeast Asia	Aquatic plant; great for mounting; used in Driftwood Water Garden.	Freshwater. Low to medium light. Ideal temperature range 68°F–82°F.
Moss	haircap, rock cap, cushion, sheet		Great for terrariums, kokedama, and tray gardens.	Even moisture. Bright indirect light.

PLANTS FOR YOUR HOME

NAME	COMMON NAME	NATIVE TO	FEATURES AND USES	CARE
Muehlenbeckia	mattress vine, wire vine, angel vine	New Zealand and Australia	Delicate but durable vine; great for Concrete Vine Planter, Lush Vertical Garden, and Single-Dowel Plant Hanger.	Water evenly. Medium light. Prefers humid conditions; temperatures 35°F–95°F; ideal is 65°F–75°F.
Neoregelia	Many varieties	South America	Epiphytic bromeliads with bright foliage; used in the Bromeliad Stump Garden.	Keep water in the cups at all times, water base soil when dry to the touch. Likes bright light. Likes humid conditions; temps 50°F–90°F; can tolerate temperatures into the 30s (°F).
Nephrolepis exaltata	Several varieties; Boston fern, sword fern	Tropical regions throughout world	Great for vertical gardens.	Likes evenly moist soil. Medium light. High humidity; Temps 60°F–80°F.
Orchids	Many varieties		Many are epiphytic; beautiful flowers; great for mounting and hanging projects.	Consult individual care instructions at time of purchase.
Peperomia	Many varieties	South America, Central America, Africa, and West Indies	Could be used in the Living Wreath project, and great for terrarium or tray planting.	They love shallow containers and warm, humid conditions, but be careful not to overwater; they rot easily. Medium light. Enjoys temperatures above 50°F.
Philodendron	Many varieties	American tropics	Vining and nonvining—vining types great for hanging in the Lush Vertical Garden, or for the Concrete Planter; nonvining types would be good for the Bench Planter.	Allow to just dry out between waterings. Medium light, but can tolerate low light. Ideal temperatures between 75°F and 85°F; 60°F at night and should not go below 40°F. Grows best with slightly cramped roots.

IN PROJECTS AND BEYOND

NAME	COMMON NAME	NATIVE TO	FEATURES AND USES	CARE
Pilea	Many varieties; aluminum plant, friendship plant	Central and South America, Asia	Great for terrariums.	Likes moist soil; less in winter. Medium light. Likes high humidity; prefers temperatures over 50°F. Pinch new growth to encourage a fuller plant. Use African violet potting mix.
Platycerium	staghorn fern	Most from Australia and New Guinea; some from Southeast Asia, South America and Africa	Epiphytic and structural; good for mounting.	Mist and water when dry. Medium light. Prefers a humid environment; 60°F–75°F; some can tolerate temps as low as 30°F.
Plerandra elegantissima	false aralia	South Pacific	Slender serrated leaf in a dark brown, copper foliage; great for a potted plant project like the Bench Planter.	Likes medium light.
Polypodium aureum	bear paw fern	Americas	Used in the Lush Vertical Garden project.	Mist daily; keep soil evenly moist. Likes bright indirect light. Prefers temperatures between 65°F–75°F.
Rhipsalis	many varieties; mistletoe cactus	Brazil and Peru	Trailing epiphytic cactus (one of my favorite houseplants); great for mounting and hanging; used in the Rain-Forest Branch.	Keep barely moist. Bright indirect light. Daytime temps 70°F–75°F; nighttime temps 60°F–70°F.
Saintpaulia	African violet	Africa	Great for terrariums; used in the Wardian Case.	Use room-temperature water; keep soil evenly moist but never soggy. Prefers high humidity. Medium light. Prefers temperatures between 60°F–70°F.

PLANTS FOR YOUR HOME

NAME	COMMON NAME	NATIVE TO	FEATURES AND USES	CARE
Sansevieria	Many varieties; snake plant, mother-in-law's tongue	Africa	Actually a succulent; great low-maintenance structural plant; could be used in the Bench Planter.	Let dry between waterings; less in winter. Low to medium light. Keep temp between 40°F–85°F.
Saxifraga stolonifera	strawberry begonia	Asia	Beautiful foliage; good for hanging; used in the Single-Dowel Plant Hanger.	Medium bright light. Grows best in fairly cool conditions, ideally 50°F–70°F with low humidity; if above 65°F it will need higher humidity. Does not like to be pot-bound.
Schefflera actinophylla (syn. *Brassaia actinophylla*)	umbrella plant	Australia and New Guinea	Good stand-alone plant or for Bench Planter.	Likes evenly moist soil. Low to medium light. Prefers humidity and good air circulation.
Schefflera arboricola (syn. *Brassaia arboricola*)	dwarf umbrella tree	Taiwan	Great stand-alone plant or for Bench Planter.	Prefers evenly moist soil. Likes medium light but can tolerate lower light. Prefers higher humidity and temperatures above 60°F.
Schlumbergera	Christmas cactus	Brazil	Epiphytic jungle cactus ideal for mounting; nice bloom when daylight gets low in winter.	Prefers soil to be evenly moist. High light needs. Likes 50% humidity.
Scindapsus pictus 'Argyraeus'	satin pothos	Southeast Asia	Used in Concrete Vine Planter; would also work well in a terrarium or vertical garden.	Water thoroughly and allow to dry between waterings. Bright indirect light. Prefers humid conditions, keep away from cold drafts. Ideal temperature range is 65°F–85°F.
Sedum morganianum	burro's tail, donkey's tail	Southern Mexico and Honduras	Lovely trailing succulent for a hanging planter or the Planted Chandelier.	Bright light, but can suffer sunburn. Prefers 65°F–75°F and slightly cooler in winter rest. Use cactus potting mix.

IN PROJECTS AND BEYOND

NAME	COMMON NAME	NATIVE TO	FEATURES AND USES	CARE
Selaginella	spike moss	Variable climates; mostly Americas and Asia	Great for terrariums or the Living Diorama.	Needs moist soil but never soggy. Medium light is ideal; can tolerate lower light. Likes high humidity; prefers 50°F–75°F; no lower than 40°F. Use peat moss–based soil such as an African violet mix.
Selenicereus anthonyanus	zigzag cactus, rick-rack cactus, or fishbone cactus	Mexico	Fast-growing epiphyte. Great for hanging or string garden. Used in the Cholla Cactus Planting.	Can tolerate a bit of neglect. Medium light. Ideal temperature range is 60°F–77°F; no lower than 50°F.
Senecio radicans, *S. rowleyanus*	string of bananas, string of pearls	South Africa	Hanging succulent; good for Succulent String Garden, Single-Dowel Plant Hanger, or Planted Chandelier.	Water only when the soil is dry. High light needs. Can tolerate temperatures as high as 110°F and as low as 25°F; ideal temperature 70°F, cooler in winter. Use cactus potting soil mix.
Tillandsia	Many varieties; air plant	Central and South America, the southern United States, and the West Indies	Epiphytic bromeliad; perfect for mounting or crafting; used in Tillandsia Nest and Tillandsia Wall Hanging.	Water by submerging; mist to increase humidity. Medium to high light. Consult care needs for individual varieties.
Tradescantia albiflora	wandering Jew, inch plant	South America	Vine; great for Lush Vertical Garden and Single-Dowel Plant Hanger.	Keep soil evenly moist in the growing season, drier in winter. Medium light. Moderate humidity; ideal temperature 60°F–75°F. Use African violet soil mix.
Vesicularia dubyana	Java moss	Southeast Asia	Aquatic plant; great for mounting.	Freshwater. Low to medium light. Ideal temperature range 68°F–82°F.

P   R   O   J

E   C   T   S

BUILD

Sometimes you want to challenge yourself with a project that utilizes a set of skills, tools, and materials that are a little beyond the normal scope of indoor gardening. The Bench Planter was one of the most rewarding projects I made from this section because it satisfied my desire to create a simple yet functional piece of furniture that shows off a playful Ming asparagus fern. The following projects feature an array of innovative ideas for making planters using a range of materials—including wood, clay, and glass—that beautifully showcase the plants.

Bench Planter

A beautiful slab of wood can be transformed into a bench or coffee table with a built-in planter.

This bench planter can work as a bench or coffee table. Mine functions as a bench in my home's entryway. If you intend to use the piece as a bench, choose a larger vertical plant with some height—otherwise the plant becomes lost. If you're using the piece as a coffee table you should opt for a plant with a low-growth habit, like a hoya or pothos. This will keep the space where the table sits open and the room's sight lines clear. Since I wanted my piece to function as a bench, I used a Ming asparagus fern, which has a soft, airy look. Asparagus ferns are not really ferns, so they are not as demanding as a true fern and a little more tolerant of receiving less water. They require bright indirect light. If you have a spot with lower light, use an aspidistra or sansevieria. For a high-light space a ponytail palm would be a fun structural plant.

The piece of walnut was found at a lumberyard. It had a natural opening in it about 5½ inches wide, which I chose to use as the hole for the plant. I love the organic lines of the walnut and the natural opening it has, but if you cannot find a piece of wood with a natural opening you can make your own by drilling a pilot hole and using a jigsaw to enlarge the hole into an opening large enough for a plant. If you are making your own opening you can opt for an irregular circle or make a perfect circle using a compass. I used a fairly thin 1-inch-thick walnut board. Most slab benches and tables are closer to 3 inches thick. Any board between 1 and 3 inches thick will work. The bench in this project is 52 inches long, but any length between 36 and 60 inches will work.

I purchased 14-inch-long unfinished-steel hairpin legs on the Internet (see Resources); they're also available in stainless steel and in other lengths. You could use another type of leg if you do not like the look of hairpin legs.

I used a very simple 6-inch plastic pot with an attached saucer for the container. I thought the attached saucer would be handy for watering, and I liked the fact that the saucer looks like it's part of the pot. You could also use a ceramic soup bowl with a rim. The main thing to consider when selecting a pot is that it is secured to the underside of the wood slab by the rim of the pot, so whatever container you use should have a sturdy rim.

MATERIALS

Piece of wood at least 3 feet long and 1 foot wide, preferably with a natural opening for the plant (A)

Tung oil or other wood finish (B)

Four 14-inch hairpin legs (C)

14 screws no longer than the thickness of the piece of wood (D)

Wood trim that's the same width as the lip of the planter (E)

2 to 4 flat metal brackets (F)

6-inch planter with lip (G)

6-inch Ming asparagus fern (H)

TOOLS

Dust mask

Random orbital sander with an assortment of sandpaper that includes 80-, 120-, 150-, and 220-grit sandpaper (I)

2 clean rags (J)

Stain applicator (K)

Pencil

Small handsaw (L)

Drill with screw bit to fit the screws you're using (M)

Wearing the dust mask, sand both sides of the wood. Start with the coarse-grit sandpaper (80-grit) and work your way to the fine-grit sandpaper (150- or 220-grit). You don't have to sand the underside of the wood as much as the top side. I did not use the fine-grit sandpaper on the bottom side at all, only on the top.

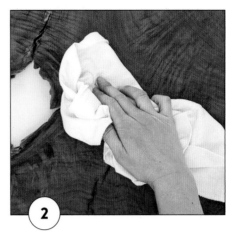

Wipe the dust off the top and bottom sides of the wood with a dry, clean rag, then wipe them again with a damp rag. Wipe the wood several times until there is no dust left and your rag comes away clean.

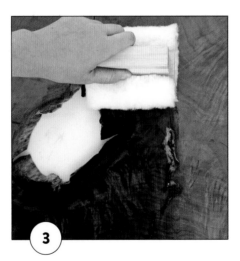

Apply the tung oil or other finishing oil to both sides of the wood with a clean stain applicator according to the manufacturer's instructions.

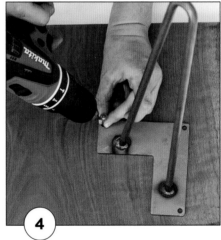

With the top side of the wood slab facing down, position the hairpin legs so that they're each an equal distance in from the slab's four corners. Mine are 2 inches in from the long sides of the slab and 4 inches in from the ends. Mark the holes where the screws will go with the pencil. Predrill pilot holes ¼ inch deep and then drill in the screws.

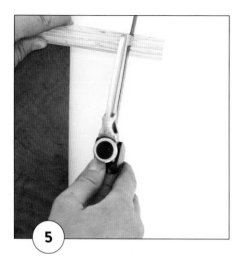

5 Use the handsaw to cut two 1-inch-long pieces of wood trim. If the container you're mounting is smaller than 6 inches you will only need 2 pieces. If you're using a large or heavy pot, cut 4 pieces of wood.

6 Place the container over the hole so that the opening of the container and the opening in the wood are aligned.

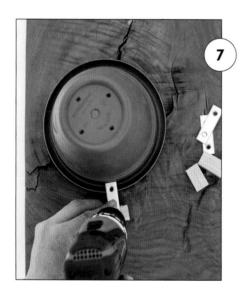

7 Predrill a hole in the center of each of the pieces of wood trim so that they don't split. Then place a metal bracket over the wood and the lip of the container, lining up the hole in the wood and metal bracket. Drill in the screw so it goes through the wood trim and into the table. Make sure the bracket is screwed on tightly enough to securely hold the lip of the pot to the wood, but loose enough to swing it aside when you want to remove the container for watering. Repeat with another piece of wood and another bracket on the opposite side of the container. If you're using 4 pieces of wood, repeat two more times so that there's a piece of wood and a bracket evenly spaced around the lip of the container.

8 Remove the asparagus fern from its pot. Turn the table over and place the asparagus fern in the container.

WATER

You can water the fern in place if you are careful not to splash water on the bench (wipe up any splashed water immediately). If you would like to remove the plant to water it, simply reach underneath the bench, hold the bottom of the container with one hand and rotate the metal pieces with your other hand until you feel the container drop. Pull the container and plant down through the hole. The Ming asparagus fern prefers evenly moist soil, but can tolerate dry periods. They like a higher level of humidity, but it is not a must for survival. You can mist them to give them more humidity.

LIGHT

Bright indirect light is best for Ming asparagus ferns. Direct sun will burn the plant, and insufficient light will cause it to turn yellow.

TEMPERATURE

Asparagus ferns prefer daytime temperatures between 70°F to 75°F and nighttime temperatures between 60°F to 65°F.

MAINTENANCE

The wood slab will need to be recoated with tung oil or another finish from time to time. If the wood looks thirsty and has a dried-out appearance, remove the planter and reapply the tung oil or other finish to the wood.

Concrete Vine Planter

Make your own concrete built-in planter with built in support for a climbing vine.

Concrete is a durable medium and easy to work with. Concrete's contemporary look is often associated with modern design and architecture, but I feel that it lends itself to almost any style. This concrete planter is a good example. Its simple bowl shape makes it an ideal project for getting started with concrete. The shape is formed using an oversize bowl as a mold, and a dowel is built in for the vine to climb up. You can use any metal, plastic, or glass container for the outer mold, which will form the shape of the pot, but I recommend using a plastic container for the smaller inner mold, which forms the opening for the plant.

I used a philodendron called satin pothos, which has beautiful white spots and silver-green foliage. Philodendrons are a great choice for the small opening in this planter because they do not mind their roots being a little tight. A mattress vine would also work well.

The concrete is easiest to work with when the temperature is between 50°F and 90°F. In general, if the temperature is not pleasant for you, it's not going to work for the concrete. It is also good to work outdoors if possible for ventilation, for optimal safety wear safety glasses and dust mask.
Use a cork plant mat or felt pads under the planter once the project is completed to prevent scratching if you are placing the planter on wood, glass, or another scratchable surface.

MATERIALS

Approximately 30 lbs. of premixed dry
  concrete mix (I used Sakrete) (A)

Cooking oil or spray-on oil (B)

36-inch dowel with a ⅜-inch diameter (C)

Approximately 1 cup of small gravel (I used
  dark pea gravel) (D)

4-inch potted satin pothos (or another
  vine) (E)

TOOLS

Safety glasses

Dust mask

Gloves (F)

3- to 5-gallon bucket (G)

Paintbrush (H)

Wide metal or plastic bowl with a 12-inch
  diameter (I)

Garden trowel (J)

1-quart plastic container (K)

Half a wine cork (L)

2 or 3 clean rags

1

Wearing safety glasses, gloves, and a dust mask, and following the manufacturer's directions, mix the dry concrete in a bucket with water until a wet mudlike consistency is formed. Add the water a little at a time, so that you don't add too much and end up with a mixture that's too watery.

2

Using a paintbrush and cooking oil or a spray such as Pam, oil the inner part of the large bowl and the exterior of the plastic container.

3

Scoop the concrete into the bowl to within an inch of the top of the bowl. You might have some concrete left over; discard it in the garbage (don't pour it down a drain or sewer—it will harden and clog the pipes). Shake and knock the bowl gently to eliminate the surface bubbles; this will also help level the surface of the concrete. If the surface isn't level after you've shaken the bowl, use a trowel to level it.

4

Determine where you'd like to position the hole for planting the vine and place the cork in the center of that spot. (I set my vine off center.) The cork will create the drainage hole for the planter. Use the plastic container to press the cork down into the concrete until the cork hits the bottom of the bowl.

5

Weigh down the plastic container with the small stones. (Later, the stones will be used for the planting.)

6

Insert the dowel into the concrete an inch or two away from the inner container. Set the bowl on a level surface and let the concrete dry for 24 to 48 hours. I always let it dry for longer than 24 hours. A good way to tell that the concrete is dry is when the color has changed from dark to light and it feels dry to the touch.

7

Once the concrete is completely dry, remove the inner mold by gently rocking it out of place. Rotate the large bowl onto its side and gently pull the concrete pot out, using the empty planter space for leverage. If the planter has rough edges and you wish to smooth them, use a metal file or stone to gently rub them off. Even though the concrete is dry, be careful with it because it will still be susceptible to chipping for a few days. If there is any debris in the drainage hole remove it gently with a chisel. Clean the surface of the concrete, wiping it first with a wet rag and then with a dry rag.

Plant the vine in the hole and top dress with the gravel you used to weight down the inner mold.

WATER

Place the planter in a sink or tub to water the vine. Put it back in place once all of the water has drained through. Water thoroughly and allow to just dry between waterings. Cut down on watering in winter. Satin pothos prefers a humid environment, so supplement watering with misting, or place it on a tray of gravel, near a humidifier, or in a humid location.

LIGHT

Place in bright indirect light, but not in direct sun.

TEMPERATURE

Satin pothos prefers temperatures of 65°F to 85°F.

FERTILIZER

Feed satin pothos as little as once and as often as twice a month spring through fall with a 20-10-10 liquid fertilizer diluted by half.

PROPAGATION

Take 4-inch tip cuttings of the satin pothos in spring or early summer and insert them into moist peat moss–based potting mix.

Cactus Clay Garden

These handmade pinch pots create a cohesive collection for displaying small cacti.

Topped with white sand, these white-on-white creations make an elegant winter windowsill garden. This project uses bake-at-home polymer clay to make small, hand-formed vessels for cacti. Once the pots were shaped, I used materials like linen, burlap, plastic, and crumpled paper to make impressions along the sides of the pots, giving each its own texture and pattern. The quirky, individual style of the pots makes them the perfect handcrafted gift.

I selected cactus plants that had a mostly white color scheme. If you are in a climate where temperatures drop at night, be sure to move the plants away from the window until the sun has risen and the window has warmed up. You could also use a collection of haworthia and gasteria or ferns. If you do use ferns don't display them on a windowsill—ferns burn in direct sun.

Use caution when you're working with cacti—they shouldn't be handled without protective gloves, or use tweezers or folded paper to hold them.

MATERIALS

1 pound of oven-bake polymer clay (A)

Four 2- to 4-inch cacti (B)

Succulent and cactus soil mix (C)

White aquarium sand (D)

TOOLS

Parchment paper or a nonstick oven mat (E)

Rolling pin (F)

Two ³⁄₁₆- or ¼-inch strips of bass or balsa wood (G)

Smoothing tool (such as a clay modeling tool) (H)

Materials for printing patterns and texture, such as burlap mesh, fabric, paper, plastic flowers, or other materials (I)

Brass tube with a ¼-inch diameter (J)

Baking sheet (K)

Utility knife

Gloves, large tweezers (L), or a folded sheet of paper (for handling the cacti)

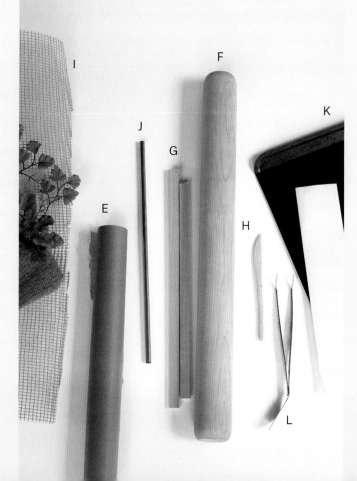

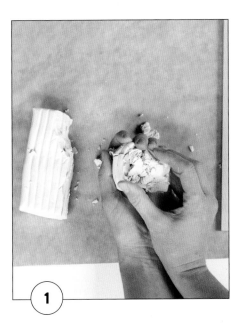

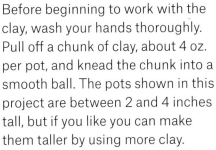

Before beginning to work with the clay, wash your hands thoroughly. Pull off a chunk of clay, about 4 oz. per pot, and knead the chunk into a smooth ball. The pots shown in this project are between 2 and 4 inches tall, but if you like you can make them taller by using more clay.

Lay the parchment paper or oven matt on the work surface and place one balsa strip on each side. You'll use the balsa strips to rest the rolling pin on to create an even layer of clay.

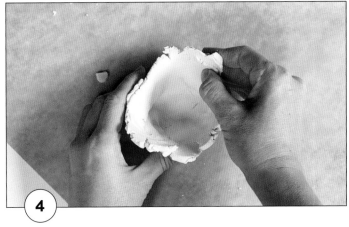

Use the rolling pin to roll out the clay into a rough circle that's between ⅛ and ¼ inch thick. If you'd like the pot to have a sturdier upright structure, then roll the clay to ¼ inch thick.

Pull the edges of the circle of clay up and gently begin to form it into a potlike shape. Pinch together the over-lapping folds and smooth the folds together with your fingers or a smoothing tool. If you'd like the pot to have a smooth rim, use a utility knife to slice off any ragged edges. While you're smoothing the folds be sure to brace the other side of the wall with your fingers so that you don't rip or stretch the clay.

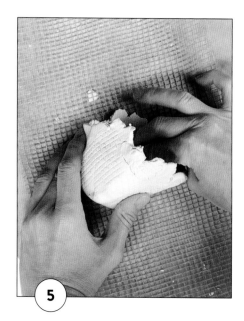

5

Place the material you wish to use to imprint a pattern on the side of the pot on the parchment paper. (In this photo, I'm using burlap mesh.) Holding the pot from the inside, press the outside of the pot into the material. Repeat around the outside of the whole pot. You can cover the pot completely with imprints or space them apart.

6

When you have formed a shape you are happy with and applied the pattern, place the pot back on the sheet of parchment paper and level the base if it's uneven. Using the brass tube, poke a drainage hole in the base of the pot. Line a baking sheet with another piece of parchment paper, place the pot on the baking sheet, and bake as instructed on the polymer clay package.

7

Once the clay pot has cooled place a layer of cactus soil in the bottom of the pot.

8

Wearing gloves or using a pair of tweezers or a folded piece of paper wrapped around the cactus, place the cactus in the pot. Fill in the sides with additional soil if needed to fill the container.

9 Top dress the soil with white sand.

WATER

It is easy to overwater cacti, so be sure the plants need water before you water them. The best way to know when your plant needs water is to familiarize yourself with how heavy a just-watered plant feels versus a dry plant. The dry plant will weigh considerably less. When you do water make sure you water well. Less frequent, but more thorough waterings are better for the plant. Allow the plants to dry out between waterings. When plants are growing and blooming they need more water, but during colder months they need very little water.

LIGHT

Give your cacti the sunniest window you have. Indoors, they need at least four to six hours of strong light daily. You will know your plants are not getting adequate light if they begin to stretch toward the light.

FERTILIZER

Use a diluted liquid fertilizer formulated for cacti and succulents once or twice a year during the growing season (spring and summer).

Staghorn Fern Shadow Box

A mounted stag-
horn fern makes
a splendid display
for either a shelf
or wall.

Staghorn ferns are amazing plants that are often mounted on flat boards or planks. An epiphytic fern, staghorn ferns have two distinct leaf forms: small, flat leaves cover the root structure and take up water and nutrients, and green, pronged fronds emerge from this base. The pronged fronds can reach 3 feet in length. Don't remove the brown, flat leaves at the base of the plant—these are essential.

My home is short on wall space, so I wanted to make a staghorn fern mount that could rest on a shelf. This take on the traditionally mounted staghorn fern is versatile: by creating a shadow box the mount can function as a freestanding display for either a shelf or a wall.

You can build your own shadow box or find an old box to reuse for this project. Choose a rot-resistant wood such as cedar, cypress, or redwood. The best time to mount a staghorn fern is in spring, at the beginning of its growing season. If you wanted to substitute another plant you could use an epiphytic orchid or rabbit's foot fern.

MATERIALS

Sphagnum moss

11- × 11-inch-square piece of
water-resistant wood (for the back of the
box) (A)

An additional piece of the same wood that
can be cut into four pieces to make the
sides of the box (B)

12 small nails or screws (C)

Staghorn fern (D)

Green sheet moss (E)

Sphagnum moss (F)

Clear monofilament fishing line (G)

Two screws (optional; for hanging the box)

16-inch (approximately) length of wire
(optional; for hanging the box)

TOOLS

Large bowl (H)

Saw (I)

Tape measure (J)

Hammer (K)

Drill (L)

¹⁄₁₆-inch drill bit (M)

Scissors (N)

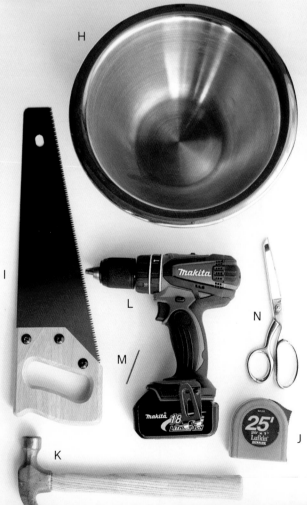

1

Place the sphagnum moss in the bowl and fill it with water until the sphagnum moss is fully immersed. Soak the sphagnum moss in water for at least an hour.

2

If you are constructing the box, cut the wood to size. You can also have a lumberyard cut it down for you.

3

Make the box. Using a hammer and nails (or a drill and drill bit), attach an 11- × 4-inch side piece to the 11- × 11-piece of wood. Attach the side piece to the back piece at each corner. Attach the other 11- × 4-inch side piece to the opposite side of the back piece. If you are using old wood that splits easily, predrill pilot holes to start the holes for the nails or use screws instead of nails—they won't crack the wood as easily. Attach the two longer side pieces using four nails (or screws) for each side. Attach the longer sides to the back piece of wood at each corner and then attach toward the front to the neighboring side piece; this will stabilize the front of the box.

4

Place the fern in the box in a spot you find visually pleasing. I set my fern off center.

5

Set the fern aside. In the spot where you want to position your fern, drill a circle of holes through the base of the box that is between 1 and 2 inches larger than the diameter of the base of the fern you are mounting. The holes should be about 1 inch apart. For example, if you are using a 6-inch potted fern, you would drill a circle of holes that is 7½-inches in diameter.

6

Squeeze the water out of the sphagnum moss. Reserve a small amount of moss to use in step 9, and make a nest out of the rest of the moss in the middle of the circle of holes.

7

Pull the fern out of the pot and use your fingers to remove any excess soil from the root ball.

Place the fern in the nest of sphagnum moss and pack more sphagnum moss around the fern's root ball.

Place the green sheet moss over the layer of sphagnum moss (it is just for additional color until the fern grows over the moss).

Begin wrapping the fishing line around the moss. At the back of the box, tie a knot in the fishing line that's too big to fit through a hole and thread the fishing line through a hole. Wrap it around the moss and thread it back through another hole.

Continue threading the fishing line through the holes and around the moss until the moss is securely tied to the back of the box. Avoid drawing the fishing line over the plant itself. Once the fern and moss are secured, thread the fishing line through a hole to the back of the box and tie a snug knot so that the fishing line doesn't slip back through the hole.

OPTION If you wish to hang the shadow box, drill a screw into the back of the side pieces of wood. (Don't screw them into the back of the box; the wood is too thin and the screws will pop through to the front.) Secure a wire from one screw to the other and use the wire to hang the mount on the wall.

WATER

To water, soak the mounted fern in a sink, large basin, or tub. Use room temperature water and soak the fern for 10 to 15 minutes to be sure that the root ball is saturated. Another option is to water the root ball with a hose or watering can, again with room temperature water. Let the water drain and the staghorn fern dry a bit before returning it to the shelf or wall. Water regularly throughout the growing season, and water more frequently as the temperature rises. The chief concern with indoor staghorn ferns is a lack of humidity; they should be misted frequently (at least once a day) and given ample ambient humidity during the warm growing season.

LIGHT

Staghorn ferns like bright light, but not direct sunlight. They can handle more sunlight if they're given enough water, warmth, and humidity.

TEMPERATURE

The most common staghorn fern, *Platycerium bifurcatum*, is native to Australia and can survive nearly freezing temperatures, but they thrive in warm, humid conditions.

FERTILIZER

Feed your staghorn fern up to once a month with a balanced water-soluble fertilizer during its active growing season with a solution that's diluted to one half the recommended solution. Suspend fertilizing during the dormant season.

PROPAGATION

Once your staghorn fern has grown large enough, you can propagate it by division. The best time to divide a plant is in early spring. To propagate your plant, untie the fishing line and remove the plant from the mount. Use a sharp knife to cut between rhizomes and include at least two leaves in each division plus a bit of the root ball. Pot the new divisions individually and keep them warm and moist until they begin to grow independently.

If your staghorn grows small pups—the plantlets at the base of the fronds—they can be removed once they are at least four inches wide. Cut them off with a sharp knife, wrap their roots in sphagnum moss, and mount them.

Single-Dowel Plant Hanger

This simple, lightweight plant hanger is made out of a single square dowel.

I am always on the lookout for crafty new ways to hang plants. There often seems to be a shortage of hanging pots and ready-made hanging systems available at garden stores, and most of the hangers are large and clunky without much in the way of style. This lightweight, delicate plant hanger is made out of a single dowel, which you can find at most craft and hardware stores, and it will hold any pot with a lip. I used an aged Terra-Cotta pot with a strawberry begonia. The round green-and-silver leaves of the strawberry begonia have a red-hued underbelly that looks wonderful against the terra-cotta's patina. I love strawberry begonias, or *Saxifraga stolonifera*, but their common name is a bit of a misnomer as they are not true begonias. They are called strawberry begonia because their basic leaf structure is that of a true begonia and they spread by runners, just like a strawberry plant does. A hoya or aeschynanthus would also work well for this project.

If you would like to age your own terra-cotta pot, you can do so with either lime or moss. The lime will give the terra-cotta a white cast, while the moss will give it a green look. To age the pot using lime, combine garden lime and water together in a 50-50 ratio and stir until the mixture has a pastelike consistency. Paint the mixture onto the outside of the pot and let it dry. Once it's dry, sand the mixture off the pot in random spots for a more natural look. Then spray the pot lightly with two or three coats of clear enamel top-coat. Spray the inside of the pot as well to prevent water absorption into the pot. Work in a well-ventilated area with gloves and a face mask. If you would like a mossy, green look, age the terra-cotta using

moss and yogurt. Simply soak the pot in water, paint with yogurt, and rub with moss. Set the pot in a damp, dark, cool place for a week to a month, until moss begins to grow on the surface of the pot, giving it an aged appearance.

MATERIALS

5-inch pot with rim (A)

8 to 12 feet of 1mm waxed string (B)

36-inch square bass, balsa, or poplar wood dowel with a ⅜-inch width (C)

Strawberry begonia or another plant to fit in pot (D)

TOOLS

Tape measure (E)

Saw (F)

Drill (G)

¹⁄₁₆-inch bit (H)

One or two clamps—if you do not have clamps you can substitute rubber bands (I)

Wood glue (J)

Scissors

Measure the inside diameter of the pot at the bottom of the lip by holding one end of a piece of string on one side and drawing it across to the other side. Measure the length of the string.

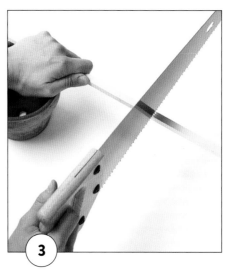

Measure the thickness of the pot's lip and add the two measurements together—the length of the string and the thickness of the pot's lip. The result will give you the length for two of the balsa wood pieces, allowing the frame to fit snugly directly below the lip. To determine the length of the other two pieces of wood, double the width of the dowel and add that number to the sum of the length of the string and the thickness of the pot's lip.

Using the saw, cut the balsa wood dowel into four lengths, based on the measurements you determined in step 2.

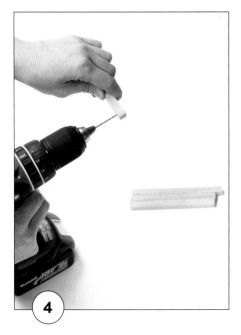

4

Drill a hole through the two longer pieces of wood, near the end and in the middle of each piece.

5

Apply some wood glue to the ends of the two shorter pieces of wood, and press them onto the longer pieces of wood to make a square.

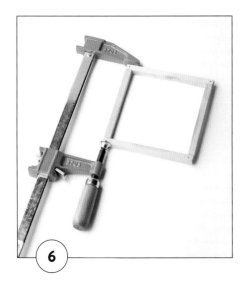

6

Use a clamp to hold the wood pieces together while the glue dries. If you don't have a clamp, use rubber bands or string. Let the glue dry completely.

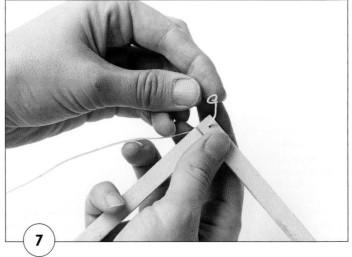

7

Cut four pieces of string a little longer than the length you would like the planter to hang. (I used lengths of 24 inches.) Pull one length of string through each hole in the wood hanger, and tie knots on the back side. The knots should be double knots or larger so that they don't slip back through the holes. Make sure the knots are secure by tugging the string on the other side. Gather the four strings together at the top and tie them together for hanging the pot.

8

Place the pot in the frame and hang the frame.

WATER
Remove the pot from the hanger and water in the sink, allowing the water to drain fully before replacing the pot in the hanger. Strawberry begonias like a fair amount of water during their growing season (spring and summer). Try to avoid getting their leaves wet, because they are susceptible to fungal disorders. Water them less frequently during winter, when growth will also slow.

LIGHT
Strawberry begonias like bright but not direct sunlight. Be careful of exposing the plant to too much heat and humidity.

FERTILIZER
Use a diluted, balanced, water-soluble fertilizer a few times during the growing season.

REPOTTING
You should repot your strawberry begonia every spring, as these plants do not like to be pot-bound. If your plant starts to look a bit bare in the center it may be time to propagate new plants from the mother's offsets.

PROPAGATION
To propagate simply place the plantlets from the runners into soil without removing them from the runner. You can place the offshoots back into the same pot as the mother or put them in their own pot next to the mother. Within a month the plantlets will develop their own roots and you can snip the runner to separate it.

Planted Chandelier

Found materials and small trailing succulents can be combined to make a charming chandelier.

With this project I wanted to capture the softening light of a late summer day and bring it in for the cold and dark season to come. This chandelier adds the romance of a warm blanket on a cool autumn evening to any room. It is a free-spirited creation, made with a found branch, old glass yogurt containers, some ball chain, tea lights, and one *Senecio radicans*. Senecio is an easy-to-grow succulent that makes a wonderful hanging houseplant. Other plants that would work are *Senecio rowleyanus*, *Ceropegia woodii*, rhipsalis, or *Sedum morganianum*. For the hanger, I used an old branch that was the base of a shrub that had died. The wood had been drying for a few years, so it had a nice aged look. It works well because it has multiple branches and is well balanced. You could also use something like a bicycle wheel or other metal object in place of the wood. When you hang the glass jars from the wood, arrange them so that their weight is evenly distributed along the hanger so that the branch (or other object) they are hanging from remains level.

MATERIALS

A found branch or other object with an interesting shape (A)

Eyebolt (B)

3 feet of chandelier fixture chain (C)

30 feet of antiqued-brass beaded-ball chain (D)

8 to 9 small glass jars (E)

Antiqued-brass connectors for the beaded-ball chain (F)

6-inch *Senecio radicans* or other small hanging plant (G)

5 battery-operated tea lights (real tea lights may be used, but use them with extreme caution due to fire danger) (H)

TOOLS

Drill (I)

Drill bit that matches the size of the eyebolt (J)

Wire cutters (K)

Pliers (chain pliers if you have them) (L)

Predrill a hole in the top of the branch, or in the spot you'll be placing the eyebolt. I recommend holding the branch lightly to find its natural balancing spot, and pre-drill the hole in that spot.

Screw the eyebolt in the hole you've predrilled.

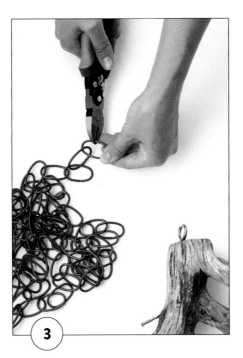

Using the wire cutters, cut the length of chandelier fixture chain that you'll need to hang the chandelier from the ceiling.

Attach the chain to the eyebolt and use the pliers to close the gap in the link.

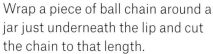

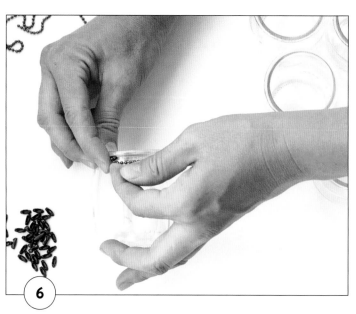

Wrap a piece of ball chain around a jar just underneath the lip and cut the chain to that length.

Attach a connector to one end of the ball chain, wrap the chain around the jar under the lip, and attach the other end of the ball chain to the other side of the connector, so that the chain is secured to the jar. If it is really hard to get the ball chain in the second end of the connector, open it a bit with the pliers, but be sure to close it completely once you have secured the chain.

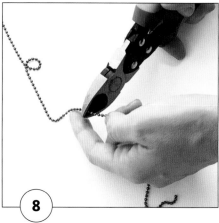

Make a handle from which to hang the jar. Loop a piece of ball chain about the same size as the one you just made between the jar and the already attached ball chain. Attach a connector to the end of the second ball chain and then to another ball about eight balls up, or as close to the first end as you can. Repeat this on the other side of the jar, so that you've made a loose handle across the top of the jar. Repeat steps 5 through 7 with the remaining jars.

Cut a length of ball chain, between 6 inches to 15 inches (so that the jars hang at different lengths), for each of the jars you're using.

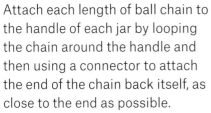

Attach each length of ball chain to the handle of each jar by looping the chain around the handle and then using a connector to attach the end of the chain back itself, as close to the end as possible.

Break the senecio into four parts. Plant each part in a jar.

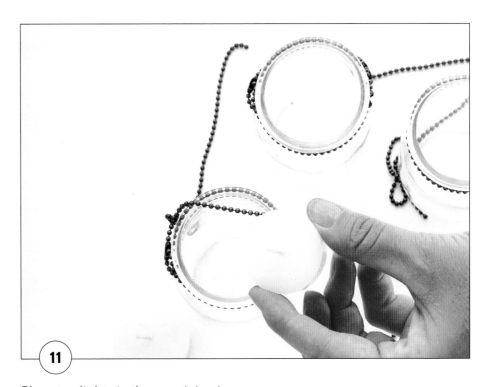

Place tea lights in the remaining jars.

12

Attach all of the hanging jars to the branch in various spots by wrapping the ball chain around the branch and using a connector to attach it back to itself. Check periodically during the process to see how the weight of the jars is distributed across the branch. The chandelier should be balanced and hang evenly when you are finished.

WATER

Let the senecio almost dry out between waterings, and water them less frequently during their dormant season (fall and winter). The glass jars do not have drainage holes so be careful not to overwater them. If you put too much water in the jar and see water pooling at the bottom you can gently turn the jar upside down and allow the water to run out of the jar. Be alert to any signs of mold; if you do notice mold developing remove the plant from the jar, clean the jar thoroughly, and replant the plant using new soil.

LIGHT

Indoor senecios prefer very bright indirect light. Avoid hanging them near air conditioners and radiators.

FERTILIZER

Fertilize during spring and summer one to two times with a general houseplant fertilizer diluted by one half the recommended solution.

Lush Vertical Garden

Create your own easy-to-maintain lush vertical garden. ——

The first time I saw one of Patrick Blanc's vertical gardens in Paris I stopped dead in my tracks. His awe-inspiring gardens have been the inspiration for countless vertical gardens. One of the challenges of installing a vertical garden in your home is the weight of the garden's soil and frame. In this project the weight of the garden is decreased by not filling the frame with soil, but rather just hanging the potted plants from a ⅛-inch-thick sheet of plywood. This 4- × 2-foot panel is still heavy, but not nearly as heavy as a traditional vertical garden panel. The larger obstacle in installing a vertical garden in your home is usually irrigation, but for this panel the need for an irrigation system or for watering the garden while it's still on the wall is eliminated. The plants can be easily removed one at a time from the wall and watered in a sink. This also has the advantage of allowing you to easily change out a plant or redesign the vertical garden at any time.

I used lush bear paw ferns, Peruvian grape ivy, and a diagonal line of cordatum lemon philodendrons for a pop of lemon-lime green. You can use different plants, but be sure to choose plants that have the same light needs. They can have different watering needs, since you can remove and water them individually, but the light requirements should be the same for all the plants. You should select plants that are full and drape well; for example, tradescantias, *Chlorophytum comosum*, or any philodendron.

When you mount the piece on a wall be sure to hang it from at least two points so that it stays balanced. You will also

want to make sure the screws are inserted into the wall's studs, or else use heavy-duty drywall anchors so that the weight of the piece is supported. I suggest hanging the plywood on the wall while it's empty and then hanging all the plants on it after it has been secured.

MATERIALS

Two 4-foot-long garden stakes with a ¾-inch-thick width (A)

2- × 4-foot × ⅛-inch-thick piece of plywood (B)

10 wood screws (C)

Felt pads (optional; to prevent the piece from scratching the wall)

Roll of 18-gauge galvanized wire (D)

Fifteen 6-inch plants with similar light needs (E)

TOOLS

Pencil (F)

Tape measure (G)

Saw (H)

Drill (I)

¹⁄₁₆ (or larger) drill bit (to make the holes for the wire) (J)

Wire cutters (K)

Drill bit matching the size of your screws (L)

Pliers

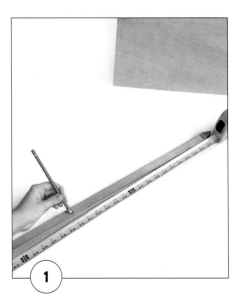

Make the frame for the back of the plywood. Line up the two garden stakes with the points facing the same direction and draw a line with your pencil across the two stakes at the spot where the stakes taper into a point. Then, measuring from the top of the stakes (the end that's not pointed), draw a line across both stakes at 30 inches from the top. You should now have four lines—two on each stake.

Cut the two stakes at the two points you have marked. You should have four pieces—two that are 30 inches long and two that are about 18 inches long. Each pair should be exactly the same length in order to make a perfectly rectangular frame for the back of the box. The frame will be attached to the plywood and prevent it from resting directly against the wall, which will create a gap for the wire to sit in without scratching the wall.

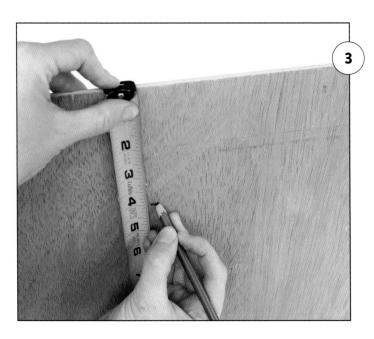

On the back of the plywood, measure and mark the spot that's 4 inches from the top (the long side) and 9 inches in from the side (the short side). Repeat this on the remaining three corners of the plywood. These marks will be your guides for attaching the garden stakes to the back of the plywood. If you like, for additional guidance, make several marks at 4 inches from the top and bottom and several marks at 9 inches in from the sides. Your measurements might be slightly different if the length of your garden stakes is different.

4

Predrill two holes in all four stakes, one hole at each end, about 3 or 4 inches from the end. You'll use these holes to screw the garden stakes to the back of the plywood.

5

Starting with one of the long stakes, screw it to the back of the plywood, aligning it with the marks you made. Use a tape measure or ruler to make sure that it is straight. Then attach the two side pieces (the shorter stakes) and the bottom piece to make a rectangle. Be sure that the stakes are tightly attached to the plywood by applying pressure to them while you screw them on so that you end up with a tight connection. If you are hanging the garden on a wall that may get scratched by the frame, attach a few felt pads to the frame.

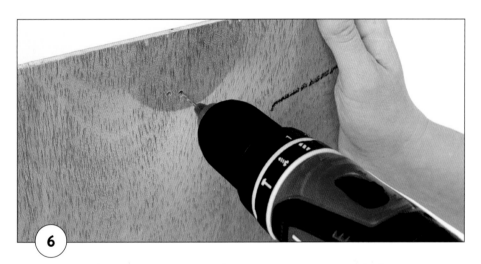

6

About 3 inches from the top and 5 inches from the sides, use the ¹⁄₁₆ drill bit to predrill two holes next to one another, less than a ½ inch apart. Continue along doing this making a roughly five across, three down pattern. You should have fifteen pairs of holes.

Cut a 22-inch length of wire and, from the front side of the plywood, thread each end through a pair of holes.

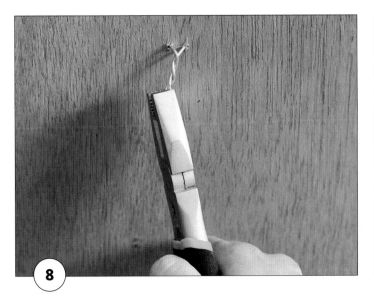

Pull about an inch or two of wire through each hole. You should have a loop of wire on the front side. Place a 6-inch pot in the loop while holding the two ends of wire on the other side. Pull the wire through the holes until the pot is secure, with the wire under the lip of the pot, and secure the wire by twisting the ends together snugly with pliers. Once the ends are twisted together, bend them toward the back of the plywood so that the wire doesn't poke out. You can also cut off any extra wire. Continue along all fifteen pairs of holes. As you move along to the next pair of holes, you can remove the plants from the wire loops—it's easier to finish making the wire hangers and to hang the plywood while the hangers are empty.

Once you have secured all fifteen of the circular hangers, install a wire hanger from which to hang the whole board. I used two screws inserted in opposite ends of the top piece of the back frame (the frame made of garden stakes), and then I strung a wire tightly between the two screws. You could also use a picture hanging kit. Once the plywood is hung on a wall, insert the plants into the wire hangers.

WATER

To water the plants in this display you simply pull the individual pots out of their wire hangers and water them in a sink or tub trug. The ferns require more water and humidity than the philodendron and cissus. I mist the ferns daily. Water each potted plant individually when it feels dry and lightweight. The ferns will need water at least once a week, the others will need to be watered less often, but of course this will vary depending on the plants you selected, the humidity and temperature of your home, the time of year, and the region you live in.

LIGHT

Use plants that need the same amount of light—the plants I used all need bright indirect light.

MAINTENANCE

You may need to occasionally prune the plants, remove dead leaves, replace a plant, or reconfigure them.

CRAFT

From willow branches to dried flowers to foraged specimens, many of the projects in this section rely heavily on dried botanicals and natural materials that are put to use in unexpected ways. One of my most treasured works of art featuring preserved flowers is Flowers on a Wall. I love the scale and changeability of this project. I continue to add and change out the dried flowers I used in the project every few months, keeping it fresh and new.

Flowers on a Wall

A striking work of art created out of dried botanicals seems to float on the wall above this desk.

One of my favorite artists, Jim Hodges, uses artificial flowers pinned to the wall in his piece *Changing Things*. His delicate and poetic art is a reflection of the frailty of life and a freezing of time. His work was an inspiration in the creation of this project.

The flowers for this project are real, not artificial, but they're dried in sand for two weeks and mounted on a wall using dressmaker pins. You can dry just about any type of flower in sand, but certain flowers will be a little more fragile. I used flowers collected from the garden and meadow near my home: California sunflowers, two clematis 'Madame Julia Correvon' and 'Etoile Violette', nasturtiums, hellebores, Queen Anne's lace, and rose campion. Flowers like poppies and nasturtiums can be used, but they're delicate, so they need to be removed from the sand very carefully. Other flowers that dry easily include evening primrose, hydrangea, roses, sweet peas, pansies, violets, zinnias, echinacea, delphinium, hollyhocks, yarrow, thistle, cornflower, bachelor buttons, nigella, anemones, calendulas, daisies, and craspedia. I dried my flowers in batches—it reduced the amount of sand and number of boxes needed for drying.

Since the flowers will be attached to a wall with dressmaking pins that will be hammered into the wall, you'll want to think about the overall picture you want to make before picking up a hammer. You can make any pattern you like, using as large or small of an area as you like. Be creative: make a grid, a random drift, a nebula, or small cluster. I did a fairly large

spray that used around 100 flowers. I also varied the depth of the pins that the flowers are mounted on, so some of the pins are hammered in closer to the wall, and others jut out to further emphasize the three-dimensional nature of the piece.

In order to maintain the appearance of the dried flowers, this project should be installed in a room with low sunlight—the darker the room the flowers are in the longer they will last. The room should also have low humidity. If you place dried flowers or leaves in a room or spot exposed to moisture they will rehydrate and wilt—the flowers will remain attached to the pins, but the look of the piece will change significantly.

MATERIALS

Horticultural or aquarium sand

1 or 2 sturdy cardboard boxes or large plastic bins (I used 11- × 14-inch boxes) (A)

50 to 100 fresh flowers (B)

Large sheet of paper (optional)

Dressmaking pins (C)

Super glue (D)

TOOLS

Chopstick

Small paintbrush

Painter's tape (E)

Hammer (F)

1

Pour a ½-inch layer of sand into the box and spread it out evenly.

2

Put the flowers face down on the sand, and gently pour more sand around and over them until they are completely covered. Use the end of a paintbrush or a chopstick to provide some support under the petals as you pour sand over them. The additional support can prevent the petals from breaking off from the weight of the sand falling on them. Leave the ends of the stems sticking out so you can locate the flowers when you come back to retrieve them. Set the box aside for two weeks for the flowers to dry.

3

After two weeks, uncover the flowers one at a time. Begin by brushing away sand with a small paintbrush until you can see the outline of the flower. Continue to gently brush away sand until the flower can be lifted out. If you feel resistance while lifting the flower, stop and remove more sand with the paintbrush.

4

Gently remove any excess sand with a small paintbrush. Set the dried flowers aside and continue removing the remaining flowers from the sand.

(5)

(6)

Arrange your flower design. Lay the flowers on a large piece of paper on a flat surface first, rearranging them until you have a composition that you like with regard to the colors and sizes. Give each flower a number. (If you don't have any paper, you could also lay the flowers on a flat surface or table and use small pieces of paper or painter's tape to place numbers next to them.)

Apply small pieces of painter's tape to the wall in the same arrangement that you've made out of your flowers, and number them to correspond with the numbers of the of the flowers, so that you'll know exactly which flower will go where. Applying the painter's tape to the wall will also give you a sense of what the finished design will look like. You can work in sections if the wall area is bigger than your tabletop workspace.

(7)

Mount the flowers, varying the depth of the pins to emphasize the project's three-dimensional nature. There are two ways of mounting the flowers on pins. Some flowers are soft enough to push a pin through the center, while others will fall apart. A good way to know if you can push a pin through a flower is to test the flower. Often very thick or hard-centered flowers, such as Echinacea, will be hard to stick a pin through. Also, if the flowers are too delicate they might break apart (for example, clematis will fall apart). If you are not able to push a pin through the center the other option is to glue the flower to the pin once the pin is hammered into the wall.

MOUNTING WITH GLUE

A. Hammer the pin into the wall to the desired distance.

B. Put a spot of super glue or super glue gel on the tip of the pin or on the back of the flower.

C. Place the flower on the tip of the pin.

D. Gently place painter's tape across the top of the flower to hold it in place until the glue has dried. You must remove the tape slowly in order to not tear the flower petals.

MOUNTING WITH PINS

A. Push the pin through the flower's center.

B. Pull the flower to the lower part of the pin and gently hammer the pin in the wall with the flower at the bottom of the pin.

C. Once the pin is secure pull the flower to the top of the pin until the tip of the pin disappears.

TIP You may have to adjust your design as you go along. Feel free to add or subtract flowers as needed. If the flowers are exposed to any humidity or sunlight you will need to periodically replace some of them.

MAINTENANCE
The flowers in this display will not last forever. As they fade or wilt or begin to look tired you can refresh part or all of the display with a new set of dried botanicals.

Anthotype Photograms

Ephemeral photographic prints made with extracted botanical juice and the power of the sun echo the transitory character of gardens.

Anthotype photograms are a perfect reflection of a garden's ever-changing nature. An anthotype photogram is an image produced by placing an object directly onto a surface that has been made light-sensitive by coating it with a photographic emulsion. The emulsion used here is made from plant materials. This results in a delicate, color-infused, low-contrast print. Anthotypes by nature are temporary—they might last from six to eight months—and part of the charm of an anthotype is watching the image fade away over time. Some people scan their artwork to make a permanent record of it, others store their prints in a dark place to extend their longevity. I like to display them and enjoy them for as long as they last. If you are going to display your anthotype photogram put it in a spot with no direct sunlight and if possible use UV-protective glass when framing it. If you wish to display them in a room that receives a lot of light, plan on replacing them every six months.

This project calls for using spinach leaves to make an emulsion, but you can use all kinds of petals, leaves, and berries to make emulsions. Some plant emulsions can take weeks to develop; spinach leaves have a relatively short processing time, making them a perfect introductory emulsion. Other flowers, vegetables, and fruits that you can use to make emulsions include pansies, which make a beautiful shade of deep purple in one to two weeks; marigolds, which make a light rusty yellow in three to four weeks; cabbage, which makes a purple hue in two to three weeks; onion skins, which make a rich orange in three to four weeks; and beetroots, which make a fuchsia in two weeks.

When you use paper with deckle edges it is nice to see the edges in the final framing. I used 7- × 9½-inch paper with 8½- × 11-inch frames, with a mat board behind the print and a slightly smaller piece of foam core in between the mat board and print, so the artwork floats and you can admire the torn edges of the print.

MATERIALS

3 sheets of heavyweight watercolor paper (I used 100% cotton rag fiber, 7- × 9½-inch handmade, deckle edge, 150-lb. white paper from Papeterie Saint-Armand) (A)

Approximately 4 cups of raw spinach (you can use regular or baby spinach) (B)

3 small trees or plants for making the photograms (I used *Zelkova serrata*, *Juniperus pingii* 'Loderi', and *Microcachys tetragona*) (C)

Three 8½- × 11-inch frames (D)

TOOLS

Painter's tape (E)

Mortar and pestle, blender, or food processor (F)

Cheesecloth (G)

Measuring cup or bowl (H)

Foam brush (I)

Towel (J)

Piece of glass larger than the paper used to make the print (you can use the glass that comes with the frame) (K)

On each sheet of paper, just in from the deckle edge, run a length of painter's tape along the border but leaving the deckle edges uncovered. Smooth the tape down once you have it in place. Repeat along all four edges of each sheet of paper. This will give you a uniform white border.

Grind or blend the spinach until it is completely processed and looks like coarse pesto.

Transfer the pulp to a doubled-over piece of cheesecloth.

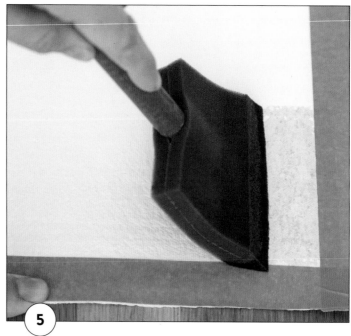

4 Hold the cheesecloth over a bowl or measuring cup, and squeeze the cloth until all the liquid is extracted into the bowl.

5 Using the foam brush, coat the paper with the spinach emulsion, brushing from side to side in long, continuous strokes. Place the paper on a flat surface in a dark place and let dry. The drying time will vary depending on the temperature of your home—it could take about ten minutes to an hour.

6 While the paper is drying, pull the plants out of their pots and remove as much soil as you can by gently combing through the soil with your fingers.

7 Run water over the roots of the plants to rinse off all the dirt.

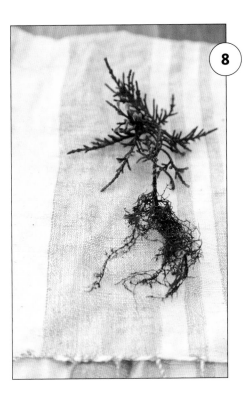

Place the trees on a towel and let them dry until there is no moisture left. While the tree roots are drying, check on the paper.

If the emulsion is dry coat the paper with another layer of emulsion, but this time brush the emulsion on from top to bottom. Return the paper to a dark place and let dry.

Once both the paper and plants are dry, position each plant on a single sheet of paper and cover each with the glass. The plant will compress into a two dimensional object.

11 Place the glass-covered print in the sun and wait 1 to 4 hours. Monitor the changing color of the print. Once the paper is very light green and significantly lighter than the area under the plant, remove the frame from the sun and remove the plant.

12 Remove the tape from the edges and frame the print.

Fall-Foraged Garland

**A seasonally
inspired garland
for a fireplace
mantel or table
centerpiece.**

Fall is the perfect time to create a garland out of foraged materials. The changing season and colorful foliage always inspire me to craft with foraged materials, especially if I want to make something for a family get-together. Use this garland to dress your mantel or as a table centerpiece for a party or Thanksgiving.

Instead of using traditional autumnal colors, I opted for shades of pale blue, pink, burgundy, and lavender. The color palette, while still seasonal, offers an alternative to fall's usual warm reds and oranges. I layered foraged materials, a final garden harvest, and a few living succulents. I harvested amaranth, rose hips, and California pepper berries from the garden, collected lichen, oak branches and seed pods from western redbud trees and then added a selection of succulents: echeverias, aeoniums, and sempervivums. If you want to bring in more orange and red you could opt for bittersweet, pomegranates, or Chinese lanterns. Tillandsias could be substituted for succulents. Fragrant branches from eucalyptus or rosemary sprigs would be another option in place of the lichen and oak branches. The California pepper berries and lichen dry without changing color. The oak leaves will turn brown, but will still look nice. The succulents can be planted outside after using them in your garland if you live in a temperate climate.

I made two different sections so that the garland could be displayed on a mantel with a work of art. This display can last for weeks. Measure your mantel or table before you begin—the length of the garland should be determined by

the length of the mantel or table on which you are going to display it. Once you know what length you'd like the garland to be, look for a large branch that is about that size or two smaller ones that can be used together.

MATERIALS

5 to 7 small-leafed tree branches (I used valley oak) (A)

Lichen or eucalyptus

Garden materials with color (such as amaranth, rose hips, and California pepper berries) (B)

Succulents such as aeoniums, echeverias, and sempervivums (C)

Twine or 22-gauge florist wire (D)

Floral tape (optional)

1 to 2 large lichen-covered branches (E)

TOOLS

Clippers (F)

Scissors (G)

Wire cutters

1 You will work in sections, making little bouquets that you'll attach to one of the branches. Start with a small leafy branch, and place a long strand of lichen on top, weaving it through the leaves and letting it drape down.

Next, place a strand of the California pepper berry on the branch, allowing it to also drape down. Continue holding the stems of everything you are layering in with your other hand.

Continuing to hold the stems together, place bits of grass, amaranth, and rose hips along the branch. Set the bouquet aside.

Pluck the succulents out of the soil and cut off the roots. Slip a length of wire high through the base of the succulent. Pull the wire through so there are equal lengths of wire on each side of the base of the succulent. Fold the wire down so that the wire becomes the stem, and twist the two wire pieces together. For a really sturdy connection, you could use floral tape to cover the wire, wrapping the tape down to the end of the wire.

Add the succulents to the bouquet and wrap wire around all of the stems, including the wired succulents at the base, two to three times to secure the stems together.

6

Attach the bouquet to one end of the larger lichen-covered branch by wrapping wire around both the branch and arrangement and twisting the wire snugly to secure the two together.

7

Continue to make small bouquets and attach them to the branch over the wire of the last bouquet attached to the branch. Work your way down the branch until the whole branch is covered. If you are only using one branch, work from both ends of the branch until the bouquets meet in the middle. The last bouquet you attach should be formed like a nosegay so that the stems and wire are hidden from view, wrapped underneath the bouquet instead of on the side, and then attached as the final section of the garland.

Tillandsia Nest

Welcome the natural world into your home with this handcrafted tillandsia-filled nest.

This is an easy, fun project that is great for kids. The nest is a simple creation made out of forage—dried materials you can find in your yard, along the side of the road, or in any field or forest. I used a selection of pine needles, dried grasses, old hay, lichen, vines, dried leaves, and a few seed heads. Make sure some of the materials you use are pliable, like pine needles, shredded redwood bark, horse hair, or thin vines. These materials will make it easier to form the shape of the nest. The tillandsia nest can be displayed on a tabletop or in a vase, or mounted on a branch that's hung on a wall. The tillandsia nest will last for as long as the tillandsias live. For a temporary display, use rosette-form succulents like aeoniums and wire them into the nest to keep them stable.

MATERIALS

Foraged dry materials such as old hay, pine
  needles, shredded redwood, grasses,
  vines, and leaves (A)

3 to 6 small tillandsias (B)

Lichen (C)

Branch (optional) (D)

20- or 22-gauge aluminum wire (E)

Clear monofilament fishing line (F)

Vase (optional)

Rocks (optional)

TOOLS

Small bowl (no more than 4 inches in
  diameter) (G)

Clippers (H)

Wire cutters

Scissors (I)

Gather twigs, supple grasses, vines, pine needles, etc.

Turn the bowl upside down and form a small mat of dried materials on the base of the bowl. Alternate the direction of the materials as you place them on the base of the bowl. Long pieces that hang over the bowl are okay—they'll eventually be pushed down onto the side of the bowl.

Push the longer pieces down over the side of the bowl and, using the more pliable materials, begin weaving them into the longer pieces, using the bowl as a mold to create the side of the nest.

Slowly weave the strands together around the bowl. Add new materials and work your way down to the rim of the bowl. You want the materials to vary and to become a sturdy mass. Ideally the nest should be ½ inch to 1 inch thick.

5 Once the nest feels stable and you have worked your way down to the rim of the bowl, lift the nest off the bowl and turn it over. Gently tuck in a few dried seed heads and strands of grass around the edge of the nest.

6 If you are using the nest as a tabletop display this is the last step. Place the tillandsias in the nest and you are finished! Go on to the next steps if you'd like to mount the nest on a branch.

7 To mount the nest on a branch, find a spot on the branch where the nest can sit naturally. Cut a 6-inch piece of wire and poke it through the base of the nest and around both sides of the branch to the back of the branch.

8 Hold the nest and branch together and turn them over. Twist the two strands of the wire together at the back of the branch.

9

Find another crook on the branch to place a tillandsia. Place a piece of lichen in the crook.

10

Cut a 4-inch piece of wire and bend it into a V.

11

Weave it through the bottom few leaves of the tillandsia.

12

Place the tillandsia over the lichen and bend the wire around the branch.

13 Twist the two strands of wire together. Repeat steps 9 through 13 a few more times along the branch.

14 If you are using a vase, place the tillandsias in the nest and then place the branch in the vase. If the branch is top heavy, place some rocks in the vase to prevent it from tipping over.

15 If you want to create a wall-mounted display, tie a length of fishing line to two different spots on the branch. You will be hanging the branch from the center point of this line, so find a spot where the weight of the branch is balanced.

WATER

Remove the tillandsias from the nest to water them. Tillandsias can be misted, dunked, or soaked, but I recommend soaking. It is the most thorough way to water your air plants. Place the air plants in a bowl of water for an hour or so once a week to water. They can be misted to add humidity, but unless you are very diligent they will never absorb enough water to live with misting alone.

LIGHT

Tillandsias like very bright indirect light for most of the day, with a little direct sun.

FERTILIZER

Tillandsias should be fed with a water-soluble solution. A fertilizer for epiphytes or orchids can be used.

MAINTENANCE

Remove dead leaves by cutting or pulling them off in the opposite direction of the growth.

PROPAGATION

Once an air plant has bloomed the plant will slowly die. Before it dies it usually produces offsets, or pups. If you would like to remove a pup from its parent plant, firmly hold the base of each plant and pull the pups apart from the plant.

Threaded-Leaf Wreath

A small versatile wreath to make any time of the year.

This project uses the technique behind making a garland but transforms the garland into a modern wreath. The most common type of lei or garland is made by piercing the materials with a needle and stringing them on thread. Often you see carnations, marigolds, plumeria, jasmine, or roses strung together in this fashion. Abandoning the traditional needle and thread, I used floral wire as the needle and thread to create this wreath, which adds strength and stability to its shape.

I used sage green manzanita leaves to make this wreath. Manzanita grows wild in the western United States. The tough leathery foliage is an ideal material for this wreath, because its pointed roundish leaves dry perfectly in place. A suitable alternative would be eucalyptus, which is widely available at florists.

Give this small wreath as a gift, in the tradition of the lei, at a housewarming or at a holiday gathering. The versatility of this wreath is due to its size and neat appearance. The petite nature of this wreath, at just over seven inches, allows it to be displayed just about anywhere. The leaves start out fresh, but dry over time and remain attractive. I've had one up for almost a year and it still looks great.

MATERIALS
Fresh manzanita or eucalyptus branches (A)
22-gauge florist wire (B)

TOOLS
Pruners (C)
Needle-nose pliers with wire cutters (D)

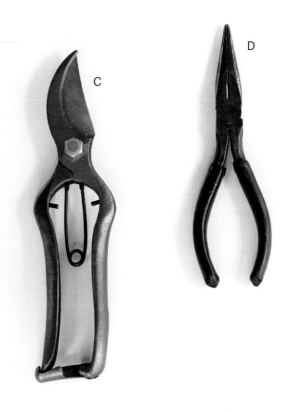

Using the pruners, cut the leaves off the branches, leaving the stems attached to the leaves. Once you've amassed one pound of leaves you'll have enough to begin constructing the wreath.

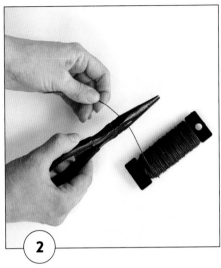

Cut a length of wire about a foot long.

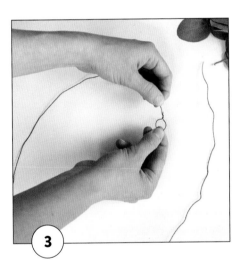

Make a loop at one end of the wire and twist the end back around the wire a few times to secure it.

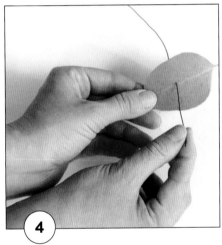

Begin threading the leaves onto the wire. Poke the wire through the center of the leaf. Face the leaves in the same direction—there will be one side that is the front. Keep the stems pointed in the same direction, but you can also adjust them later. The wreath looks best when all of the stems face inward. Continue threading the wire through the leaves until you can make a tight circle of leaves with at least a 7-inch diameter.

5 Pull the wire tight and twist it around the looped end with the needle-nose pliers in order to securely close up the wire circle. The loop functions as a hook to hang the wreath from or to hang a ribbon from.

6 Straighten any leaves that have flipped over in the wrong direction.

Willow Spheres

Celebrate the art of willow crafting by making willow spheres that can be used as light fixtures or displayed as indoor sculptures.

Willow is a sustainable, fast-growing resource that has been used throughout history to make everything from houses, fences, baskets, furniture, and fish traps. The willow industry declined with the advent of manmade products, but today there is a growing interest in willow weaving and basketry in the form of willow sculpture, wattle fencing, and garden structures. What better way to enjoy one of the oldest-known crafts than to bring a little of that willow inside?

There are many different varieties of willow that will work for this project. Willow that is grown commercially is pruned in such a way that the plants produce long, straight, flexible rods. Whether you choose to cut your own or buy them, the willow branches you use for this project must be freshly cut, not dried. It is easiest to work with willow in early spring, just before the new leaves pop. Willow branches are pliable and easy to manipulate at this time and there aren't leaves to remove. If you are harvesting your own willow, test the willow's flexibility before gathering it to make sure it will work for the project. If the willow snaps when you bend it to a 45-degree angle it will be a challenge to work with. When working with willow many crafters make their own willow cordage to use while weaving, but we are going to skip that step and opt for hemp cord, which is available at craft, art, and bead stores. There are many ways to weave a willow ball—you can use a standard basket weave or a random in-and-out pattern. This project uses a free-form pattern, which will give you more flexibility in the creation of your first willow sphere. All willow ages over time, turning a slightly more gray color.

Once the spheres are complete you can choose to display them on the floor as a sculptural installation or hang them. A light bulb on a cord or a string of lights can be used inside the willow spheres to turn the project into a light fixture. If you're using the spheres as a light fixture, I recommend hanging the sphere from its own wire or cord—don't use the electrical cord to hang the sphere.

Willow branches that are 4 feet long will make a sphere that is roughly 18 inches in diameter; a 5-foot piece will make a 22-inch sphere. If you do not have branches that are that long you can use two shorter pieces to make the length of a single longer piece. You can vary the number of branches you use to make the spheres—the more branches you weave in the denser the appearance. I kept mine light and airy, using roughly twenty stems per ball, slightly more for the larger sphere and slightly less for the smaller sphere. I made a total of three spheres, one each at 22 inches, 19 inches, and 16 inches.

MATERIALS

Willow branches (at least 20 stems per sphere and at least 3 feet long) (A)

Hemp cord or florist wire (B)

Light bulb or string of lights (optional)

TOOLS

Pruners (C)

Scissors (D)

1

If you are working with willow that has leaves, use the pruners to clip the leaves off the willow branches, clipping them off as close to the branch as possible.

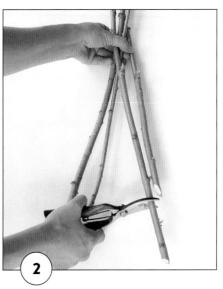

2

Cut all the willow branches to the same length.

3

First you will make a set of three wreathlike structures. Begin by cutting six 4-inch lengths of hemp cord (or florist wire, if that's what you're using).

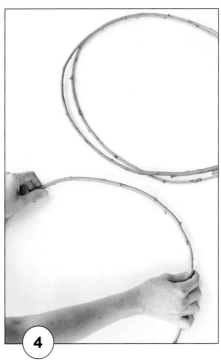

4

To create more flexibility and a rounder shape in the willow branches, gently bend each willow branch into a circle, working your way along the length of the stems.

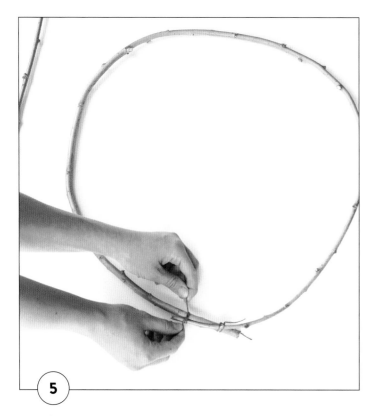

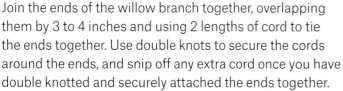

Join the ends of the willow branch together, overlapping them by 3 to 4 inches and using 2 lengths of cord to tie the ends together. Use double knots to secure the cords around the ends, and snip off any extra cord once you have double knotted and securely attached the ends together.

Once you have completed three circles join them together in a ball-like shape. Use a piece of cord to secure the rings together at the bottom and top of the sphere.

Weave a branch through the side of the sphere to stabilize the shape, threading the branch under and over the other branches. Use more cord to secure this piece of willow at two or more points along the way.

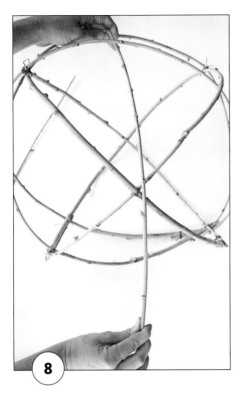

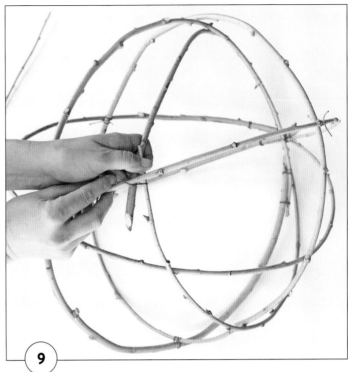

Weave branches throughout the sphere at random spots.

At first you will need to use cord to secure the branches to other branches. Once you have built up the sphere the branches will stay in place by themselves, as the sphere becomes more rigid. The longer your willow branches are, the more stability they will offer.

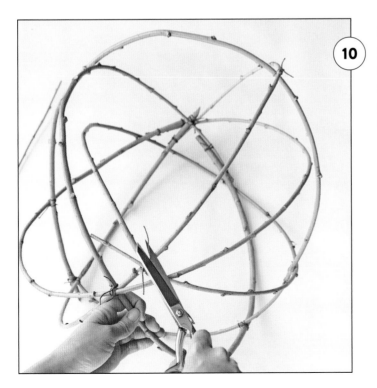

Once you are finished inspect the piece for dangling cords or willow ends that stick out too far. Clean up and trim anything that needs trimming, and then the sphere is ready to display.

Tillandsia Wall Hanging

Driftwood and a few tillandsias make a light and airy wall hanging or mobile.

This tillandsia wall hanging was inspired by today's bohemian ceramic and fiber artists, who are bringing macramé and weaving back from the 1970s, but with a modern twist. Tillandsias are the perfect plant for this project—their simple beauty and ability to grow without soil lend themselves beautifully to a wall hanging. I placed my finished piece near the entry of my house, but it could also be installed over a window as a curtain or above a bed as a mobile. Large dried botanicals would also work well for this project. If you do use tillandsias, make sure they get enough light. Tillandsias need a lot of bright light, and a little sun is welcome. If they do not receive enough light they will just limp along and eventually die.

I wanted to incorporate the weather-beaten wood of the California coast, but often it is not advisable to use driftwood from the sea in a garden because of the amount of salt in the wood. Be sure to cure the wood if it has come from the sea. If you have access to lake driftwood, that's a better option—it is ready to use right off the shore.

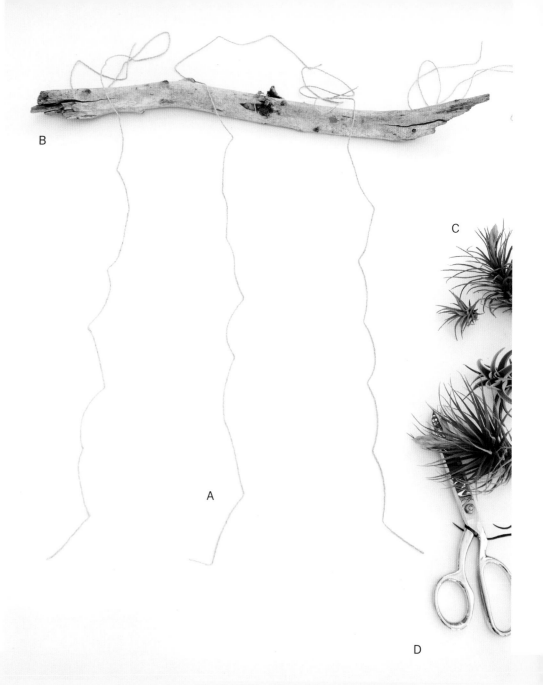

B

C

A

D

MATERIALS

8 feet of string (I used 1 mm hemp cord; any cord you find attractive will work) (A)

Piece of wood, about 2 feet long (lake driftwood is preferable, but sea driftwood is fine if it has been cured) (B)

11 tillandsias no larger than 3 inches (C)

TOOLS

Scissors (D)

1 Cut four lengths of string—two lengths at 2½ feet long and one slightly shorter than 2½ feet (these three are for hanging the tillandsias), and one to use to hang the wood.

2 Lay the branch, strings, and tillandsias on a work surface, placing the wood at the top and three strings down from the wood. Arrange the tillandsias along the lines of the string until you have an arrangement that you like (don't attach them to the string yet). For a balanced hanging, use four tillandsias on the outside strings and three on the middle string. Vary the order of the size of the tillandsias and the angle at which you place them.

(3) Begin tying the tillandsias to the string. You can start at the top or bottom of the strings and work your way up or down. As you tie each tillandsia onto the string, find a spot at which the tillandsia will be stabilized.

TYING THE TILLANDSIAS

A. You may need to attach the string in two spots to make it stable.

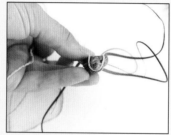

B. Tie the string around the base, if that seems best.

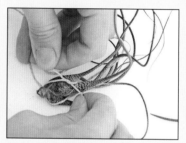

C. Or wind the string through the plant.

(4) Once you have attached all of the tillandsias, hold each string up to see how the plants hang—look at how they're spaced and the direction they face. Make adjustments if necessary, then cut off any loose threads.

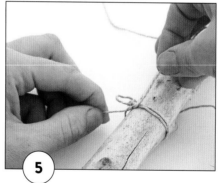

(5) Once you have attached all of the tillandsias tie each string to the wood, spaced equally part. To hang the wood, tie the fourth piece of string to the wood outside where the two side strings holding the tillandsias are attached.

WATER

I take the wall hanging off the wall and gather the tillandsias, along with the strings, and place them in a bowl of water for an hour or so once a week. Tillandsias can be misted, dunked, or soaked, but I recommend soaking because it is the most thorough way to water air plants. They can be misted to add humidity, but unless you are very diligent they will never absorb enough water to live on misting alone.

LIGHT

Tillandsias like very bright indirect for most of the day, with a little direct sun.

FERTILIZER

Tillandsias should be fed with a water-soluble solution. A fertilizer for epiphytes or orchids can be used.

MAINTENANCE

Remove any dead leaves by cutting or pulling them off in the opposite direction of growth.

PROPAGATION

Once an air plant has bloomed the plant will slowly die. Before it dies it usually produces offsets, also called pups. If you would like to remove a pup from its parent plant just hold the base of each plant firmly and pull them apart.

MOUNT

I enjoy mounting plants of all types, but one of my most loved mounting projects is the Rain-Forest Branch, which uses one of my favorite epiphytes, rhipsalis. It's a wonderful plant to work with if you are new to indoor gardening—rhipsalis's green, lush appearance belies its easy-to-grow nature. Whether they're suspended from the ceiling, mounted on a branch, or submerged in water, these projects add a dynamic focal point to any room.

Rain-Forest Branch

Add a touch of rain forest to your home with this fun, movable mounted rhipsalis.

This is a great sculptural project fashioned from rhipsalis and a large piece of a branch. The branch does not need to be hung on a wall or suspended from a ceiling, but you are welcome to experiment with those options. Or you can simply lean it against a wall or shelf.

Rhipsalis is an epiphytic cactus native to the Brazilian rain-forest canopy. It grows nestled in tree branches and drapes gracefully to the ground, and is one of a few special cacti that thrive in a tropical rain forest. This cactus has a much different appearance than its rigid desert-dwelling relatives.

The rhipsalis is wrapped and bound in the same style as the kokedama project, but the plant is then mounted on a branch to create a striking installation. Rhipsalis is the best plant for this project—it cascades down the branch and does well mounted, like most epiphytes—but you could also use a hoya or aeschynanthus (lipstick plant). Use clear monofilament fishing line to secure the rhipsalis in the moss and a wire to hold the moss-wrapped plant to the branch. This makes it easy to remove the plant for watering. If you use driftwood, be sure to cure it before installing the plant (see page 12). It is easier to work with sheet moss that has been soaked overnight—it will be more pliable and will achieve a tighter fit.

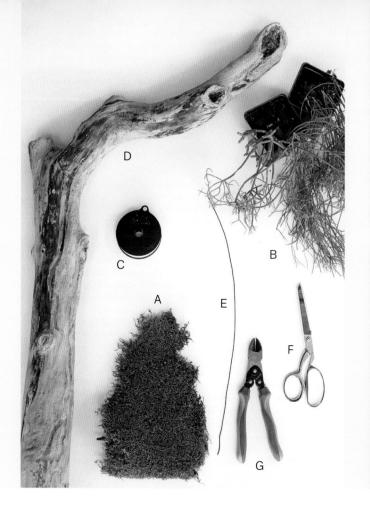

MATERIALS

Presoaked sheet moss (soak it overnight before you begin the project) (A)

Two varieties of 4-inch rhipsalis (B)

Clear monofilament fishing line (C)

Large piece of wood with a curved L-shape, about 4 feet long (D)

22-gauge florist or bonsai wire (E)

TOOLS

Scissors (F)

Wire cutters (G)

Place the sheet moss on a work surface moss-side down.

2

Pull the rhipsalis out of the pots by gently squeezing all around the pot until the plants come out with ease. Knock any loose soil off the root ball.

3

Center the two plants on the sheet moss. If it looks like you need a bit more soil, add a little bit back to the plants. You want to end up with a ball somewhere between the size of an orange and a grapefruit.

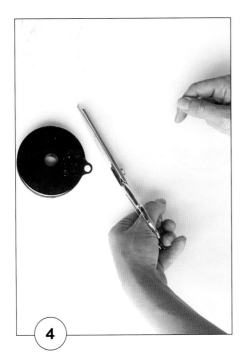

4

Cut three 5-feet-long pieces of fishing line.

5

Fold the moss around the root balls. If you have too much moss you can pinch some off.

6

While holding the moss tightly around the root ball begin wrapping the fishing line around it. Crisscross the fishing line around the moss until the moss is securely wrapped around the root ball. Be sure to wrap it tightly. If you need to wrap the moss with more fishing line cut another piece.

7

Tie off the fishing line and trim off the ends.

8

Secure the ball to the branch with wire, wrapping it tightly around both the branch and the ball one or two times. Once they're secure, adjust the ball and plants until they look like they are resting comfortably in the crook of the branch.

WATER

Gently unwrap the wire holding the moss ball to the wood. Push the ball, plants and all, into a bowl of water. Hold it underwater until air bubbles stop coming out of the moss. Remove the moss ball and plants from the water and return them to the branch once they have stopped dripping. Water frequently in spring and summer, but reduce watering to a minimum in winter. If you stick your finger in the top of the moss ball you should be able to feel if the soil is moist or not. Allow the soil to dry between waterings.

LIGHT

Rhipsalis prefers bright indirect light, due to its origins as a tropical-forest understory plant.

FERTILIZER

Fertilize a maximum of once a month with a half dilution of cactus food from April to September.

PROPAGATION

If you are interested in propagating rhipsalis, take cuttings and let the severed ends callus for a few days. Plant the callused ends in a cactus mix or sand that has been lightly moistened. Cuttings will root in two to six weeks.

Hanging Rock Garden

An unusual collection of orchids suspended on lava rocks.

For many orchids, mounting them is the most natural way to grow them. You usually see orchids mounted on wood, but mounting them on a piece of lava rock allows them to function as a hanging garden in a way that a flat piece of wood does not. A wood-mounted orchid is often displayed hanging flat against a wall, but the three-dimensionality of the lava rocks in this project allows the orchids to be suspended anywhere. The lava-mounted orchids can also be placed on a tray and not hung, if air space is limited.

Orchid species that thrive mounted are epiphytic, or tree dwelling. It is best to use a plant that will remain compact—a miniature is a great choice for this mounting project. I used a mini restrepia, a lepanthes, two dendrobiums, a masdevallia, and a trichosalpinx. Other orchids that do well mounted are cattleya, chiloschistas, angraecums, bulbophyllums, and phalaenopsis. It is often hard to find specialty orchids at your local nursery, but you can order a huge range of orchids online from Andy's Orchids (see Resources). If possible, try to do this project during a new growth period, when new roots have already started.

The growing conditions you should consider before choosing your orchids are light and temperature. Choose orchids that will easily grow in your indoor environment. If you are working with existing conditions and cannot provide a special environment, choose plants with a broader temperature range.

MATERIALS

Dried sphagnum moss (A)

3 to 5 orchids (B)

3 to 5 lava rocks (C)

Green moss or living sphagnum moss (D)

Clear monofilament fishing line (E)

Bonsai wire or twine (I used 1mm black bonsai wire because I like its smooth appearance. Twine will eventually disintegrate and will need to be replaced periodically.) (F)

TOOLS

Bowl (G)

Scissors (H)

Wire cutters (I)

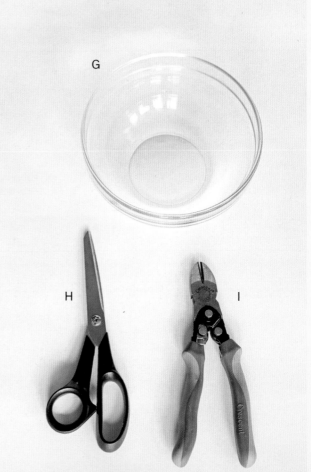

Moisten the dried sphagnum moss by placing it in a bowl of water for at least an hour.

If you are working with a potted plant, remove the plant from the pot. If you are working with a plant mounted on wood, remove the plant from the wood.

Find a place on the lava rock, such as a flat spot, for the orchid to sit. Place a chunk of moist sphagnum moss on the spot you've identified as the mount location.

Place an orchid on the sphagnum moss and add a very small dab of green moss on top of the orchid roots.

5

Secure the orchid and moss to the rock with the fishing line, wrapping the line around the rock, up, down, and over again.

6

Place the rock and orchid in the position you wish to hang them and take a piece of wire or twine long enough to hang the rock from and wrap the middle of the wire once around the rock's center (from top to bottom), twisting the wire at the top to secure it around the rock. Hang the rock, and repeat for the other orchids and rocks.

WATER

In their natural habitat orchids live on rainwater, which is low in dissolved minerals and salts. It is best to water your orchids with rainwater if you can, but filtered tap water or distilled water are also fine. The best way to water the orchids in this project is to submerge the entire plant in water. Once all the air bubbles have stopped coming to the surface remove the orchid from the water. You will probably need to water 3 to 5 times a week. If your region has low humidity and high temperatures you can expect to water at least once a day. Check the moss around the orchid—if it's dry that's an indication that you need to water. Water the orchids in the late afternoon or evening during warm months and in the morning during cool months. In between watering mist the orchids, again with suitable water. Also be careful not to use water that is too cold—it could shock your plants.

LIGHT

Refer to the tag or label that came with the plant to find out the light needs of the individual orchids you purchase. You can add growing lights to help your orchids get enough light, but be sure to pay attention to the humidity as the lights decrease the amount of moisture in the air.

TEMPERATURE

The needs of the specific plants you choose will vary; refer to the temperature range listed in the plant description. Temperature also plays a role in how much sun the orchid can take—the cooler it is the brighter it can be.

AIR MOVEMENT

Orchids need air movement. Place a fan near the hanging lava rocks to facilitate air movement. A healthy orchid that never blooms is usually suffering from a lack of airflow.

FERTILIZER

Fertilizer can be applied at a quarter strength about every three weeks, after a thorough watering.

Cholla Cactus Planting

Cacti skeletons transformed into a planter with a freshly planted display.

This tabletop planter uses a zigzag cactus mounted inside chunks of cholla cactus skeletons to make a wild centerpiece or an extraordinary display for a credenza. Or hang it on the wall for a cool vertical garden.

As cholla cacti die and decay the skeleton, or woody interior, remains intact. The skeletons can be found in flower markets, select plant nurseries, and online. They are wonderful for crafting or just displaying on their own. The trailing stems of the zigzag cactus mirror the geometric cutouts of the cholla skeletons. Other epiphytic cacti that you could use would be disocactus or an epiphyllum.

Zigzag, rick-rack, and fishbone orchid cactus are just a few of the descriptive names of *Cryptocereus anthonyanus*. The most pronounced feature of this night-blooming cactus is its long arching stems covered with serrated leaf nodes. The plant originates in the tropical rain forests of Mexico and is a tree-dwelling species. It's an ideal houseplant for a novice gardener because of how tolerant it is of a little neglect. You may want to wear gloves when handling the cactus—it has tiny hairs that can lodge in the skin and cause discomfort.

The cholla cacti chunks do not have an end that is sealed, so this project calls for sphagnum moss to be wrapped around the cacti roots in order to keep soil from falling out and to help retain moisture. Even so, there are a few precautions you should take because of the nature of the materials. Before returning the planting to a tabletop or other surface, either allow the soil to dry completely after watering the plants or

place the planting on a tray. Also, if you want to protect the surface the piece is displayed on, place felt pads or a corkboard underneath the cactus skeletons. All of the materials in this project are organic so the piece will decompose over time.

MATERIALS

Sphagnum moss (A)

3- to 4-foot cholla cactus skeleton (B)

20-gauge aluminum wire (C)

6-inch zigzag cactus (D)

TOOLS

Bowl (E)

Hacksaw (F)

Large tweezers (G)

Wire cutters

Needle-nose pliers (H)

Gloves (optional)

1

Soak the dried sphagnum moss in a bowl of water for at least an hour.

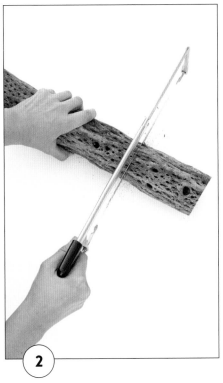

2

Using a hacksaw, cut the cholla cactus skeleton into 5 to 10 pieces that are 4 to 6 inches long.

3

If there is any debris inside the cactus skeleton pieces remove it with the tweezers.

4

Arrange the cactus skeleton pieces in a composition you like.

5

Use several lengths of wire to attach the cactus skeleton pieces together snugly at the top, stringing the lengths through openings at the top of each piece. Use the needle-nose pliers to twist the ends of the wires together and tuck them out of the way.

6

Remove the zigzag cactus from its pot and separate the individual plants.

7

Wrap the roots and a small amount of soil in the moist sphagnum moss. Wrapping the soil will help prevent dirt from spilling out of the holes of the skeleton cactus.

8

Insert the wrapped roots into the individual cactus cavities. If you have trouble fitting them in the cavity use less sphagnum moss. You can also use the back of the tweezers or your fingers to press the moss into the cavity.

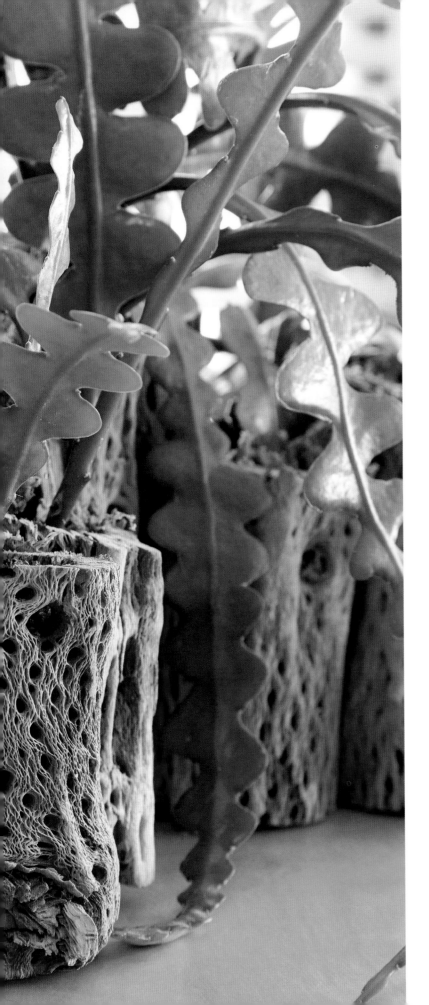

WATER

Like orchids, zigzag cactus prefers humid growing conditions, so mist it a couple of times a day to give the plants more humidity. Like many cacti it prefers to dry out in between waterings. When the sphagnum moss dries water the plants with a watering can, gently shower the whole piece, or plunge the whole construction into a tub of water. Allow the water to soak in and repeat one more time. Once the skeleton wood has dried the arrangement can be put back on display.

LIGHT

Zigzag cactus thrives in bright indirect light but can take periods of direct sun.

FERTILIZER

Fertilize with a water-soluble orchid fertilizer.

PROPAGATION

Propagation is really easy: simply take a fresh cutting and allow it to dry for a few days. Once the end has callused over insert it into a peat-moss mixture and allow to grow. During the initial growth give the new starts light moisture and indirect light.

Bromeliad Stump Garden

Let your imagination escape to a distant land by creating a magical mini landscape.

During the summer, I often find myself daydreaming about traveling to far-off places like Machu Picchu in Peru, home to countless stunningly beautiful bromeliads. Short on time and funds, instead I created a miniature garden reminiscent of that distant land. This bromeliad stump garden provides you with an escape to a faraway place without actually leaving home. The mounted plants add delightful color and texture to any space. This project takes advantage of the epiphytic nature of bromeliads by mounting them as they would be seen clinging to trees in places like Peru or Brazil.

You will want to use wood that is rot-resistant such as cypress, cedar, oak, or manzanita. Avoid using pine due to its sap. It is better to use a wood that has cured for a year or more. Do not use wood with any type of contaminant or driftwood from the sea (too much salt).

It is best to mount bromeliads during the warmer months when the plants and roots are actively growing. Use plants that are not in bloom yet, as once a bromeliad blooms it dies. It is best to mount pups because their root systems have not developed. If they're mounted as pups the plants will form a small number of hard, strong roots that just serve as holders and do not provide nutrients to the plant. When grown in soil they form large, soft root systems that provide additional nutrients to the plant. If you choose to mount a plant that has already formed the soft root system, the mount should be able to accommodate the plant's root ball. The root ball should be covered with sphagnum moss and will need to be watered regularly to continue the nutrient flow to the plant.

For some species, a layer of moss is not necessary, but neoregelias benefit from moss. During the warmer months your plants will tend to dry out a lot quicker than potted plants so be sure to give them enough moisture until they become established.

MATERIALS

2 rot-resistant logs (ideally, with naturally formed crevices) (A)

Five 4-inch bromeliads suitable for mounting (Make sure they all have the same light needs and are able to be mounted. Most tillandsias and aechmeas do well mounted, often billbergias and neoregelias can be mounted. Guzmania should not be mounted.) (B)

Sphagnum moss, either living or dried (C)

8 outdoor wood screws (D)

4 strips of nylon stockings (E)

Decorative moss (I used loose green moss) (F)

Cork for the bottom of the logs (optional; to prevent scratches) (G)

TOOLS

Hammer (H)

Chisel (I)

Drill (J)

Driving bit to match the size of the screws you're using (K)

Countersink bit to match the size of the screws you're using (if you're using hardwood) (L)

If the logs do not have a natural cavity or only have a very small cavity, use a hammer and chisel to create an opening that is just large enough to give the bromeliads a place to rest their roots.

Loosen the bromeliads from their containers and remove the extra soil from their roots. If the plants have well-developed roots, wrap sphagnum moss around the roots. Find the place where the bromeliads sit most naturally in the cavity and insert the plants. You can use 2 to 3 bromeliads per log.

Drill a screw on either side of the cavity, leaving some of the screw exposed enough to tie a strip of nylon to. If you are working with a very hard wood you may need to predrill the holes in order to get the screws to go in the log.

Tie a piece of nylon to one screw, stretch it across the bromeliads, and tie it to the screw on the other side. You may need two screws on each side, with two pieces of nylon supporting the bromeliads, with one that's higher up on the plant. The main goal is to tie the plants firmly so they don't wiggle around. This will allow new root growth to attach to the wood.

5

Hide the nylon strip by tucking decorative moss around it.

WATER

Mounted bromeliads require a higher level of humidity and a lot more water than potted ones do. In dry air, the mounted plants may fail to develop sufficient roots to attach themselves to the substrate (the wood) and their foliage may suffer from extreme dehydration. To help them live happily in your home mist them daily to provide additional humidity. You can also place a tray filled with gravel and water nearby; this will add humidity to the environment. Ideally the humidity should be 50 to 70 percent. The higher the temperature and the more vigorous the air movement, the higher the humidity levels should be.

Many bromeliad species have a central cup—you should fill the cup with water. This reservoir of water should be flushed once a week to keep it clean and free of bacteria and dried nutrients. You should also water the plant's roots. You want to maintain moist but not wet roots.

LIGHT

Adequate light is crucial for growing healthy, colorful bromeliads. The bromeliads I selected need a sunny spot indoors. Different bromeliads have very different light needs, and geographical location can intensify or diffuse the sun. Where you live also changes the level of humidity, which is related to the amount of light and water a plant needs. In a place that has a very hot, dry sun, adding more humidity is necessary. Air circulation also plays a role in a bromeliad's health. Plants that do well in the sun outdoors may burn next to an unshaded window, because of a lack of air circulation.

FERTILIZER

In their native habitat, the rosettes collect debris and rain, which contain nutrients. In a home, most of these sources of nutrition are absent so bromeliads should be fertilized, especially during the growing season. The fertilizer should be acidic. It is also very important that most of the nitrogen is in the form of ammonium or nitrate and not urea. Also, copper and boron are toxic to bromeliads. Use a complete, water-soluble fertilizer, using ⅛ to no more than ½ the concentration in the manufacturer's directions, as a full-strength dose will damage the plant. You can use it as a foliar spray or place it in the center cup of the bromeliad. Wet the bromeliads thoroughly before fertilizing them. Excessive fertilizing can cause a loss of color, leggy development of rosettes, or algae growth on the leaves.

PROPAGATION

Most species of bromeliad slowly die after blooming, but they produce one to several offsets, or pups, as they decline. Pups should be at least ⅓ the size of the parent plant before you remove them. They should not be removed until winter is over—they will develop better root systems if removed during the summer or growing season. Some pups will be easy to pull away from the parent plant, others may require a bit of force. Don't pull or twist; instead hold the pup tightly, pulling it away from the parent plant, and cut through the pup with a sharp knife. Pot the pup in ½ to 1 inch of potting mix. Brace it upright with a mini stake or a few rocks. Keep the new plant in a shady, more humid spot for a few weeks until the cut heals and the new roots begin to grow. Keep the potting mixture fairly dry until the pup has grown new roots and the cut has healed.

Driftwood Water Garden

An engaging aquatic land-scape.

This dynamic duo consists of two tall cylindrical vases, each holding a single piece of driftwood mounted with Java fern and Java moss. The ferns and driftwood are visually grounded with the addition of a few Japanese river rocks at the base of each vase. (You can find Japanese river rocks at garden shops or online.) You could use *Anubias nana* or *Anubias barteri* in place of the Java fern and Java moss. Java ferns and Java moss have low light needs, but they do require warm water. Their ideal temperature range is between 68°F and 82°F. If you do not have an ideal environment you can use a heat mat or lighting to maintain the water temperature.

I used manzanita driftwood. Mopani is also a popular drift-wood, but any hardwood will work. Only use driftwood sold for use in an aquarium—wood used for reptiles or terrariums, such as grape wood, will rot in water.

E

B

D

C

A

F

MATERIALS

2 pieces of driftwood (A)

2 tall cylindrical vases (B)

River stones (C)

Clear monofilament fishing line (D)

2 Java ferns (E)

2 pieces of Java moss (E)

TOOLS

2 small plates or other objects that will fit on top of the vases

Scissors (F)

Place the driftwood in the vase.

Fill the vase with water.

If the wood is buoyant, place a plate on top of the vase to hold the wood down. Leave the driftwood in the vase until it's waterlogged and the water is clear. Change the water every other day. On average it takes from one week to a month to season the driftwood. Once the wood is cured empty the vase. Put enough water to fill the vase in a jug or watering can and let them sit overnight. This will bring the water to room temperature and allow the chlorine to evaporate.

Place a few river stones at the bottom of the vase.

5

Cut a 6-inch length of fishing line.

6

Loosely attach the Java fern and Java moss in the crook of the driftwood with the fishing line. Double knot the fishing line and cut any excess off. When the fern and moss attach to the driftwood the fishing line can be removed completely.

7

Place the driftwood with attached plants back in the vase.

8

Fill the vase slowly with the water that was left out overnight. Repeat these steps for the second vase.

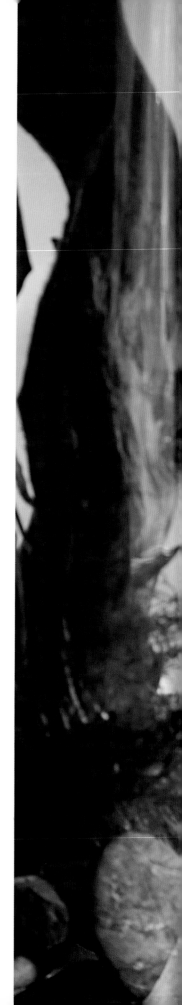

WATER
Change the water in the vases weekly using room-temperature water.

LIGHT
Bright indirect light is best; direct sun will encourage the growth of algae.

TEMPERATURE
Keep the water between 68°F to 82°F.

FERTILIZER
Use aquatic plant fertilizer.

MAINTENANCE
If algae forms on the vases gently clean it from the surface.

Lava Rock Bonsai

Lava rock bonsai are a lively take on a traditional root-over-rock bonsai.

This project is all about creating a fun yet serene tray garden. An airy *Euphorbia californica* is mounted on a porous dark lava rock displayed off center on a crisp rectangular white marble tray. The light, flutter-leafed euphorbia is set off by dark, textured lava rock and grounded by the marble tray. A surprising magenta twine holds the bonsai to the lava rock. Plants with shallow root systems work well for this project. If you cannot find a *Euphorbia californica,* or would like to use a different plant, look for a jade plant, schefflera, or ficus.

If you're working with a lava rock that doesn't have a natural depression or groove one can be chiseled or drilled very easily. Lava rock has a very porous surface that is easily chipped away.

Water your plant and rinse the lava rocks, both small and large, the day before you start the project. The rocks should be clean and not soaking wet when you work with them. The idea behind watering the plant the day before you begin the project is to allow the plant time to absorb the water and not be stressed, which will help it adapt to its new home with fewer problems.

MATERIALS

Tray or saucer (I used a 15-inch rectangular tray made of marble) (A)

1 cup of small decorative black lava rock (B)

Black lava rock, preferably with an existing hole or depression and a flat bottom so that it sits level with a tabletop (find lava rocks at pet stores or landscape supply stores) (C)

Euphorbia californica **(or other plant suitable for mounting)** (D)

Hemp twine (any color; I used magenta) (E)

TOOLS

Star drill or chisel

Hammer

Scissors

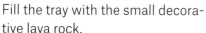

1

Fill the tray with the small decorative lava rock.

2

Find a natural depression or hole on the large lava rock for the *Euphorbia californica* to sit on. If your rock does not have a natural depression or hole, create one with a drill or chisel.

Loosen the *Euphorbia californica* by squeezing the sides of the pot, and gently remove the tree from the pot.

Gently remove any excess soil with your fingers, leaving a little bit of soil on the roots.

Plant the tree in the hole, placing most of the roots in the depression with the soil. Add more soil if needed. You can leave some of the roots exposed on the rock surface.

6

With the hemp twine, tie the exposed roots in place, wrapping the twine around the rock front to back, back to front, and side to side. Once the tree feels secure, tie a knot in the twine and cut off the loose ends. You can remove the twine once the tree has had time to grow and the roots are attached to the rock. If you opt to keep the twine, it may disintegrate over time and need to be replaced periodically. Place the plant to one side of the tray, with the curve of the tree extending out over the tray.

WATER

Water by submerging the tree in water or by pouring water over its roots. If you're watering by submerging the tree, place the entire rock under water for 10 minutes. You'll see a steady stream of bubbles as the water fills the air space in the lava rock and pushes out the air. You may need to water as often as every three days, but it should be at least once a week. When the rock mostly stops dripping, place it back on the tray with small lava rock. Cut back on the watering in winter.

LIGHT

Euphorbia californica likes a lot of light—very bright indirect light works well. A south-facing window would be a good choice.

FERTILIZER

There is very little soil in this planting, so I recommend using a diluted liquid fertilizer every week during the growing season.

Epiphyte Garden Panel

A lightweight
vertical garden
panel.

Many plants grow as epiphytes, which are an excellent choice for a vertical garden panel. In this garden panel I used a variegated vanilla orchid and Christmas cactus. Often you see or receive Christmas or Easter cactus as a small gift around the holidays. After they are done blooming, mounting them is a great way to take advantage of their epiphytic nature. Both plants need a bright spot to live. Other plants suitable in this project are hoya, rhipsalis, or, if you can find it, *Huperzia squarrosa*.

I have always loved vanilla, in anything from rice pudding and ice cream to lotions and candles. I am a sucker for its heady fragrance and sweet woodsy flavor. When I first heard that vanilla beans come from an orchid I moved this plant to the top of my must-have list. If you use orchid vines in this project they will continually reach for somewhere to root. In their native habitat vanilla orchids climb up high into trees and attach to the bark with their roots growing from their leaf joints. If you like, place a tray of soil on the floor below the panel and allow the orchids to reach the soil and grow into it. As they grow, the roots that are produced from along the stem will grow downward until they touch a suitable surface to attach to, such as soil, mulch, tree branches, or even a carpet. The plants only flower once they are mature, usually when they're at least 30 feet or longer. Vanilla blooms are small and appear in clusters only once a year. Hand-pollinating them is a tricky process—it needs to be done when the blooms open, but they only open for a day. Pollinated blooms leave behind the prized seed pods—the vanilla beans we're familiar with. I have not done this yet,

but I love the possibility. A word of caution: You may wish to wear gloves while you're handling the orchids. If the roots or stems are broken the sap can irritate your skin. If you have a reaction to the sap, wash your skin thoroughly with soap and water.

MATERIALS

Plastic plant tray (the kind that nurseries use) (A)

1 or 2 cups of orchid/epiphyte soil mix (B)

Either a contractor's garbage bag or a 2- × 2-foot sheet of black plastic that's 3–4mm thick (C)

22-gauge wire (D)

Eight to ten 4-inch coconut fiber pots (E)

Foam spray—preferably black outdoor (F)

Brick of compressed coconut fiber (G)

Silicone in either brown or black (H)

About 1 cup of green moss (I)

Two to three 6-inch vanilla orchids and six 2-inch Christmas cactus (J)

TOOLS

Utility knife (K)

Two bowls (L)

Scissors (M)

Super glue (N)

Wire cutters (O)

Safety glasses (P)

Gloves (Q)

Caulking gun (R)

Use a utility knife to cut the sides of the plastic plant tray off.

Put the orchid soil mix in a bowl and mix with water until it's saturated.

Cut the sheet of plastic to roughly the same size as the plant tray.

Use a few dabs of super glue around the sides of the tray to adhere the plastic sheet to the back of the tray and trim off any excess plastic once the glue has dried.

Make a wire hanger by cutting a 10-inch length of wire. Poke the piece of wire through the plastic sheet about 2 inches in from the side. Pull the wire through, and secure it on the front side of the plastic plant tray by twisting it tight around a cross piece on the plastic tray. On the back side stretch the wire to the other side and poke the end through the plastic sheet and secure it in the same way.

If you are using 4-inch coconut fiber pots, cut them down to about 2 to 2½ inches.

Place the coconut fiber pots at a slight angle up from the tray and, wearing the safety glasses and gloves, use the foam spray to coat the area below, behind, and around each pot to secure it to the tray. Follow the manufacturer's instructions for using the foam, and keep in mind that the foam expands. Fill in the areas between the pots with spray foam, again remembering that the foam expands. Allow the foam to set for 24 hours.

Shred the compressed coconut fiber so that you have a pile of loose fiber.

Wearing gloves and working on small areas of no more than an ⅛ to ¼ of the panel at a time, use the caulking gun and silicone to coat the surface of the foam with silicone. Smooth out the silicone with a gloved finger so that it spreads evenly.

Coat the wet silicone with coconut fiber by sprinkling it over the area and then patting it in.

Attach a few pieces of green moss with silicone to empty areas on the foam.

12 Loosen the plants from the pots and separate out each strand.

13 Carefully remove the extra soil and plant the plants in the coconut fiber pots, adding soil mix if needed.

14 Cut several small lengths of wire and bend them into small U-shaped pieces. Use them to secure the plants into the foam if they are heavy or if it seems like they need support. You may also pin in more moss if you have blank spots you want to fill. Hang the panel.

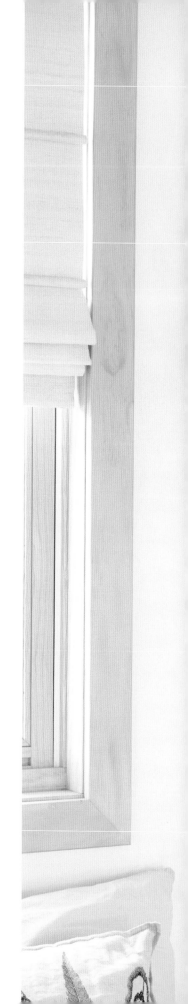

WATER

Humidity is very important for these plants. I mist my panel daily and every few days I take the whole panel down and give it a proper soak, letting excess water drain off before hanging it back up. If you have low humidity or high temperatures in summer, you will need to mist the panel at least once a day. If the moss and the area around the plants are dry you need to water. If the plants are unhappy due to low humidity, position a cool mist humidifier and a small fan nearby.

LIGHT

These plants need very bright light.

FERTILIZER

Diluted water-soluble fertilizer can be applied one to two times during the growing season (spring and summer) after a thorough watering.

PROPAGATION

If your vanilla orchid vines reach 20 feet long, take a cutting of 2 to 3 feet. Allow the cut to dry completely before planting and if possible treat it with a fungicide since newly cut divisions are prone to damping off (a horticultural disease). Snip the bottom few leaves off so that two leaf joints are buried in the fresh soil. Keep the soil drier than you normally would for the first month, but still moist to the touch.

Living Wreath

Celebrate life with a twist on the traditional May flower wreath.

One of the time-honored ways to commemorate May Day, an ancient celebration of spring, is by making a flower wreath. Instead of making a customary floral wreath, welcome the power of nature into your home with a living wreath. Although traditionally the wreath decorates a door until the day of St. John the Harvester (June 24), the idea of hanging a living wreath at any time of year is a wonderful way to celebrate life. This living wreath can be displayed on or near a front door or on a table as a centerpiece.

I used two epiphytic ferns to create a rich, green wreath. The rabbit's foot fern has beautiful lacy fronds and fuzzy feet. The sweet heartleaf fern is a dainty fern with dark green fronds that grow on dark stems. The heartleaf fern is used in the center of the wreath, while the larger rabbit's foot fern stretches along the outer edges of the wreath. When planting the rabbit's foot fern be sure to leave the furry feet exposed—the fur is actually rhizomes that need to remain exposed to take up water. The epiphytic bird's nest fern would be a good fern substitution. In place of the ferns you could opt for two types of peperomia. The heart-shaped leaves of peperomia have a variety of colors and textures and they would look great planted in a wreath.

I used a frame specifically made for living wreaths—it's available online at Topiary Art Works (see Resources). It looks like two flat wreath frames attached together with rings. This frame makes it easier to use moss and soil to support the plants and has built-in feet to bump it out from the wall. I highly recommend using the same frame.

I display my wreath outside at my home's entryway to welcome guests. This spot does not receive direct sun during the day; this is important for the ferns, which will burn in the sun. If you live in a climate that has a cold winter wait until all danger of frost has passed in your area before considering placing the wreath outside. Once nighttime temperatures drop below 60°F you should bring it in overnight. I bring the wreath indoors when the weather gets cold and display it as a centerpiece lying flat on a saucer. The saucer protects the table from the moisture and humidity of the planting.

If you have concrete walls you can hang the wreath directly on a wall inside, but I do not recommend displaying the wreath on a wall indoors if your walls are made of drywall. Even though the wreath frame has feet that push it away from the wall the moisture and humidity from the moss can stain the wall or grow mold on the wall if the wreath is displayed there over a long period of time. If you really want to display it inside on an interior wall consider making a plastic back for the wreath frame out of a plant saucer or plastic liner.

MATERIALS

Sheet moss (A)

About 1 gallon of African violet planting mix (B)

1 teaspoon water-retaining polymers (C)

11-inch living-wreath frame (D)

50 feet of 22-gauge aluminum wire (E)

Twenty to thirty 2-inch rabbit's foot and heart ferns (F)

U-shaped florist pins or florist wire (G)

TOOLS

2 bowls (H)

Garbage bag (I)

Gloves (J)

Wire cutters (K)

Pliers (L)

Large tweezers (M)

1. Soak the sheet moss in a bowl of water overnight. Squeeze out the excess water.

2. Use another bowl to mix the African violet planting mix and water-retaining polymers. Add water a little at a time until the mix is saturated and allow the mixture to rest for at least an hour.

3. Spread the garbage bag on a work surface and lay enough sheet moss on it moss-side down so that the sheet moss covers an area twice as large as that of the frame. If your pieces of moss are small, overlap the pieces so that there aren't any bare spots in between them.

Place the frame in the center of the sheet moss.

Layer the planting mix onto the frame.

Wearing gloves, pull the sheet moss up through the center of the frame and over the frame and planting mix. Then begin to pull the moss from each of the four corners up and over the frame and planting mix. Cover the frame and planting mix completely with moss, patching any area that needs more moss. It might seem a bit messy and over-whelming, but just keep going, adding moss in spots where the soil is spilling out.

Begin wrapping the aluminum wire around the moss, planting medium, and frame. Make the first loop by slipping the wire under and once around the wreath and securing the wire to itself using the pliers—it should be snug so that the loop stays in place and the wire doesn't come undone as you continue wrapping it around the wreath. Continue wrapping the wire around the wreath, leaving a finger's width of distance between each loop of wire. Pull the wire tight as you wrap and patch any spots missing moss.

8

Once you get back to where you started twist the ends together to secure the wire.

9

Loosen the plants from their containers and remove the excess soil.

10

Use the end of the tweezers or a screwdriver to pry open the moss and make a small hole for a plant. Place the roots of the plant in the hole. It may help to keep the tweezers in the hole, holding the moss open while you place the plant in the hole. Repeat with the remaining plants.

11

If the plants feel loose use a U-hook or make a V-shaped hook out of florist wire to secure them until they have time to establish themselves. Leave the wreath lying flat and away from direct light for the first few weeks so that the plants have a chance to establish themselves.

WATER

Mist the wreath daily to increase the humidity around it. Be sure to mist the feet of the rabbit's foot ferns. Do not let the wreath dry out completely. Feel the wreath and lift it to get a sense of its weight to determine when to water.

If you have a tub or bin, water the wreath by submerging it entirely in water for about 10 minutes. Remove from the water and allow it to drain before you rehang it. Or take the wreath down and gently shower it with water, then let the wreath sit for 10 minutes and then shower it again. Let the wreath drain before you rehang it.

LIGHT

Hang the wreath in a spot that gets indirect bright light. Direct sun will burn the ferns.

FERTILIZER

Fertilize with all-purpose fertilizer using about ¼ dose a few times during the growing season (spring and summer).

MAINTENANCE

The wreath will change over time and may need to be replenished or pruned. Rabbit's foot ferns can grow large, so you will need to keep them trimmed to maintain a tidy appearance.

PLANT

The art of creating a garden composition and then tending the garden can be both meditative and transportive. One of my favorite projects in this section is the Rock and Sand Landscape, which creates a miniature world with haworthias, a great easy-to-care-for indoor succulent. The ideas here range from gardens to hang or display on a tabletop to gardens that are underwater or enclosed in a terrarium—each a tiny, fascinating living world.

Miniature Flagstone Planting

**A small-scale
desert scene for a
sunny spot.**

Within Joshua Tree National Park golden rock outcroppings
and *Yucca brevifolia* proliferate. This harsh land is home to a
surprisingly diverse group of flora and fauna. Drawing inspiration from the unique beauty of the Mojave Desert, I created a
miniature desert landscape for indoors. I selected succulents
native to either South Africa or Madagascar that can grow as
houseplants. This diminutive desert oasis is reminiscent of
the Mojave, but goes beyond just re-creation—it entices the
viewer to enter and explore this miniature world of vitality.

I used a selection of euphorbia, haworthia, kalanchoe, and
crassula. The plants in this miniature garden need very bright
light with some direct sun—a south-facing window is a good
location for them. If you do not have a sunny spot, consider
substituting *Sansevieria cylindrica* or gasteria for the euphorbia. When you select plants, make sure that they all have the
same light needs and have shallow root structures. Most
succulents have shallow roots that will form a dense mat just
under the soil surface. Not all succulents do well as houseplants, and they do not all require the same amount of light.
Make sure your selection shares the same light and water
needs as well as being able to live indoors. *Euphorbia decaryi*
produces a white milky sap, called latex, that causes skin
irritation, so always wear protective clothing and gloves when
you're working with them.

Use one to two taller plants, a mid-range plant, and a few
lower-lying plants. Sometimes when you first purchase a
plant it can look like a low-growing plant, so be sure to look

at the tag or label to learn the final height of a plant when you make a selection. The tallest plant will go toward the center of the planting and the lower-growing plants around the edges, with the intermediate-height plants going to the left and right of the tallest. Use the rocks, gravel, sand, and bits of wood to give the viewer negative space to move through the composition and provide a visual resting point.

MATERIALS

Piece of flagstone about 14 × 6 inches (A)

4 to 6 felt pads (B)

Five or six 2- or 4-inch succulents for indoors: 1 to 2 taller plants; 1 to 2 medium height (I used *Euphorbia decaryi*); and 2 to 3 low-growing plants (C)

Approximately 1 cup of white sand (D)

Approximately 1 cup of crushed gravel (E)

5 to 10 rocks in different sizes (F)

Wood chunks (driftwood and found wood, for example) (G)

TOOLS (OPTIONAL)

Large tweezers (for moving gravel and rocks)

Small paintbrush (for removing loose sand)

Turn the flagstone over and place the felt pads on the bottom so that it will not scratch the surface you put it on.

2

Squeeze the sides of the pots at the bottom to loosen the plants and take the plants out of their pots.

3

Separate the larger 4-inch plants into multiple smaller pieces and remove the excess soil. The repeated forms will give instant continuity to your garden.

4

Starting on the right or left side of the flagstone, put a small amount of soil down about an 1½ inches in from the edge, leaving a border around the perimeter of the flagstone.

5

Place about ⅓ of one of the short, low-growing plants, such as the haworthia, on top of the soil, angling it so it covers much of the soil but still leans upward. You may need to prop up the plant with a rock if it is top heavy.

6

On the opposite side of the flagstone place the other low-growing plant. Tuck the roots on top of the mound of soil and cover them with soil.

7

Place half of the *Euphorbia decaryi* or another medium-height plant next to the low-growing plant. Using a little extra soil from the container you removed the euphorbia from, press down around the base of the plant, so that the euphorbia is stable in the soil. Continue planting, placing the tallest plants toward the center and low-growing plants at the edge. Leave a few empty areas for rocks and negative space.

8

Once all of the plants have been placed pour sand over the soil, using your hand as a funnel.

9

Position the gravel and any remaining rocks. I used more gravel than sand. Cover all the exposed dirt with sand, gravel, rocks, or wood chunks. If there are any bits of gravel or sand that are out of place, gently remove them with either your fingers, tweezers, or a small brush.

WATER

During winter months, when the plants are dormant, water the planting once a month. During warmer months (spring and summer), it will be necessary to water more often, probably every week. Let the soil dry out between watering. To avoid overwatering, water only enough to keep leaves from withering. If the leaves or rosettes of any of the plants shrink, pucker, or become dull they need water. The flat surface of the flagstone and the small amount of soil requires extra care when watering, so that you don't wash the soil off the planter. You can either mist heavily or gently pour water slowly from a container with a spout or small opening.

LIGHT

The succulents in this planting prefer bright light, with a little direct sun. A south-facing window works well for this project. Watch the leaves for indications that the light level is correct. An underlit succulent will begin to stretch, with an elongated stem and widely spaced leaves. If you live in an area with a dry summer or have a covered porch you may put your flagstone garden outside for the summer.

TEMPERATURE

Succulents are much more cold-tolerant than many people assume. As in the desert, where there is often a marked contrast between night and day temperatures, succulents thrive with cooler nights. Ideally, succulents prefer daytime temperatures between 70°F and about 85°F and nighttime temperatures between 50°F and 55°F.

FERTILIZER

Succulents experience their strongest growth during spring and summer. Growth slows in fall, and winter is a time of rest. Fertilize in the warmer months, a minimum of once a year and a maximum of once a month with a balanced cactus fertilizer, or once a year with a slow-release, granular, cactus fertilizer.

Succulent String Garden

The perfect hanging garden for a sunny window.

This planting takes advantage of a succulent's ability to look beautiful with little water or soil. I used two sprawling succulent varieties: variegated string of pearls and string of hearts. Both look great as a small hanging vine. If you have a bright window or sunny spot this succulent string garden will provide you with an elegant hanging garden. You could also use *Senecio radicans* or a rhipsalis. If you don't have a spot with bright light but do have a lower-light spot you could use a neon pothos.

MATERIALS

Fresh or dried sphagnum moss (A)

Three 4-inch string of pearls (*Senecio rowleyanus*) (B)

Three 4-inch string of hearts (*Ceropegia woodii*) (C)

Clear monofilament fishing line (D)

Twine (E)

TOOLS

Bowl (F)

Scissors (G)

1

If you're using dried sphagnum moss, soak it in a bowl of water until it's rehydrated (at least an hour).

2

Once the moss is thoroughly soaked, take the first plant out of its container and remove the loose soil.

3

Shape the remaining soil and roots into ball.

4

Place the sphagnum moss around the soil, covering all the exposed areas and gently patting the moss and holding it in place as you work your way around the ball.

5

Snugly wrap the fishing line around the moss, crossing it around in all directions, until the moss is stabilized.

6

Tie off the fishing line and trim the ends.

7

Cut a piece of twine at the length you wish the ball to hang. Place the ball in the center of the twine and tie the twine around the ball and secure it with a double knot. Hang the ball, and repeat with the remaining plants.

WATER

Water the plants thoroughly by dunking the balls in a bowl of water until all the air bubbles are released and the balls are fully saturated. Allow the balls to become light-weight before soaking them again. Cut back on water in winter, watering just enough to prevent the soil from drying out.

LIGHT

String of pearls and string of hearts prefer bright light with some direct sun; a west- or south-facing window is perfect.

TEMPERATURE

These are great indoor plants because they don't mind the normal, slightly dry environment most homes offer. They prefer a warm spring and summer and a slightly cooler winter. The plants may suffer if temperatures fall below 50°F.

FERTILIZER

Feed a maximum of once a month spring through fall with a balanced liquid fertilizer diluted by half.

PRUNING AND MAINTENANCE

It may be necessary to occasionally prune the string of pearls or string of hearts. Trim off any dead stems, hearts, or pearls. Pruning back the plant will promote fuller more compact growth.

The twine will need to be replaced periodically.

PROPAGATION

For the string of pearls, take a stem cutting 3 to 4 inches long in the spring and insert it into moist potting soil. Keep the soil moist until the cutting has rooted; it will root from where the leaves are attached to the stem. String of hearts can be propagated from a cutting of the tubers produced at the base of the leaves. Take the tuber with the vine attached and press it into soil. Keep the soil moist, but not wet, to encourage rooting. Once the tuber is rooted and growing in a few weeks or months, sever it from the original plant. Cuttings from the vine are best rooted with bottom heat (heat provided from a heating pad; find them at garden stores or online).

Rock and Sand Landscape

A modern min-
iature Japanese
rock garden.

A traditional Japanese rock garden uses rocks, sand or gravel, moss, pruned trees, shrubs, and sometimes a water feature to create a small stylized landscape. The sand or gravel is raked to represent ripples in water. This miniature haworthia tray garden takes its inspiration from these wonderful gardens, but does not imitate them, and in place of the carefully pruned foliage found in Japanese rock gardens, this project uses architectural haworthias.

The white sand used here emphasizes the beauty of the rocks. Choose your rocks carefully, as each one should enhance the composition—each form contributing to the overall balance. You do not have to rake the sand, but if you want a more stylized look experiment by raking it with your fingers, a fork, or a chopstick. With a tray garden you are trying to create the feeling of a place, and having a path through the garden provides a visual entry into the garden and gives the eye a space to rest.

Haworthias make great houseplants, especially for a tray garden. A small succulent originating from South Africa, they are readily available, have a range of colors and shapes, and stay relatively small. Plants range in size from 1 to 4 inches in diameter. Often succulents that remain small can be found growing under shrubs and trees in nature—they do not want the blazing sun associated with many cacti and succulents. While most rosette-form succulents need more light than an indoor

environment can provide, haworthias can tolerate more modest lighting. Because they stay
small they can comfortably fit on a table near a
window without seeming to take over a room.
Other succulents that would work for this tray
garden are jade plant or gasteria. You could also
use cacti for this project, such as a pincushion
cactus or an astrophytum.

MATERIALS

Cactus and succulent potting soil (A)

Tray with a drainage hole (I used a tray with
   a 12-inch diameter) (B)

4-inch haworthia (C)

Two or three 2-inch haworthias (C)

White sand (D)

5 rocks ranging in size from 4 inches to ½
   inch (E)

TOOLS

Small paintbrush

Bonsai brush or large paintbrush

1

Place a layer of soil on the bottom of the tray. The depth will depend on how deep your tray is; the tray I'm using here is shallow, so I used a layer of soil that was less than 1 inch deep. The layer should be deep enough to place the plants and their roots and then add more soil and the sand on top.

2

Loosen the plants from their pots and remove any excess soil.

3

Place the 4-inch haworthia to the far right.

4

Add more soil around the plant's roots.

5

Plant the two or three smaller plants grouped together on the opposite side of the tray, adding soil as needed. Smooth out the soil so that the level of soil is a little below the tray's rim.

6

Pour white sand over all the exposed soil.

7

Place the rocks on either side of the two groupings of plants, leaving an open path between the plants across the center of the tray.

8

Use a small paintbrush to remove any sand from the haworthias. Use a larger paintbrush or bonsai brush to smooth the surface of the sand, or rake the sand with the tip of the paintbrush's handle or your fingertips.

WATER

Let the soil dry out between waterings and then water thoroughly
using a watering can or faucet head
with a sprinkle spout in order to
provide a gentle flow of water. It is
better to let the plants get a little
dry than to overwater them. If any
of the sand is displaced, simply
replenish it after watering. Increase
watering in the warmer months,
decrease in the winter.

LIGHT

Haworthias like very bright light.
Indoors a little sun is nice, but they
can survive in bright indirect light. If
the plants start to stretch and elon-
gate it is a sign they are not getting
enough light. Their leaves will also
lose their color.

FERTILIZER

Fertilize the plants one to two times
during the summer growing season
with a cactus fertilizer, and suspend
fertilizing during the colder months.

PROPAGATION

If any of your haworthias produce
offsets you can remove them with a
sharp knife or snippers to produce
a new plant. Cut the offset as close
to the mother plant as possible,
including a few roots. Allow the
baby haworthia to dry out and then
repot the offsets in a small pot.
Place the plants in a warm bright
spot and water adequately.

Three-Fern Kokedama

Delight in this suspended moss and fern string garden.

Hikes through the shady ravines of Northern California, surrounded by the beauty and tranquility of the moss-and-fern-covered slopes, inspired this three-fern kokedama. This adaptation of that vibrant landscape to a ball of moss imparts a playful element to the ferns. The trio of ferns has all the wonder of nature in a delightful string garden. The light, delicate nature of the trio of ferns works perfectly in a bathroom—the green of the moss and ferns is rejuvenating and they love the humidity, bright filtered light, and proximity to water.

Kokedama originated as a form of bonsai in Japan, coming out of the Nearai bonsai style during the Edo era (1615–1868). Nearai bonsai consists of growing the plant in a pot until it's so tight the roots and soil will maintain their shape when taken out of the pot. The bonsai is then taken out of the pot and displayed. Kokedama means "moss ball," so the kokedama bonsai is a plant grown in a pot, then taken out of the pot, and covered in moss. Originally the plant was displayed on a stand, often on a plate or tray from which the moss and plant could absorb water. The contemporary form of the hanging string garden was made popular by Fedor Van der Valk of the Netherlands. He uses crocheting techniques, his own soil blends, and grass seed in place of moss. The freeing of the kokedama from bonsai tradition allows everyone to try their hand at making a moss ball or two.

I've displayed my three-fern kokedama by suspending them from a ceiling beam. Keep in mind that they need to be removed for watering, so don't put them in a place that's difficult to reach. If you are starting out with dry moss you should rehydrate it by soaking it overnight in a bowl or tray of water.

MATERIALS

Peat moss and akadama soil, in a ratio of 7 parts to 3 parts (Akadama soil is a clay used in bonsai that helps retain moisture. If you cannot find akadama use a premixed bonsai soil.) (A)

Three 4-inch potted ferns (Maidenhair, asparagus, or leatherneck are good choices.) (B)

Sheet moss (I used freshly foraged live moss. If you do not have access to live moss you can purchase live or preserved sheet moss at your local nursery or online.) (C)

White or ivory 1mm or 2mm waxed cotton cord (Waxed cotton or hemp cord is available at jewelry or craft stores in a large variety of colors. Twine or polyester cord will also work.) (D)

TOOLS

Bowl, bucket, or tub trug (E)

Scissors (F)

Mix the peat moss and akadama soil together in a tub trug, bucket, or bowl, using a ratio of 70 percent peat moss to 30 percent akadama soil. Use your hands or a spoon to mix everything together. Add water little by little while mixing until the soil is thick and sticks together when you form it into a ball.

Remove a fern from its container and gently remove any loose soil from the root ball. With ferns you don't need to remove much of the soil.

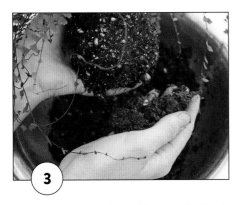

Pat a layer ½ inch to ¾ inch thick of mixed soil around the root ball, and gently shape the mixture into a ball.

Wrap the sheet moss around the ball, moss side out. Completely enclose the soil and press the moss into the ball of soil.

Cut a piece of cord at least 5 feet long. Lay the cord out, and place the bottom of the moss ball on the cord at the halfway point, at 2½ feet from one end.

6

Wrap the cord around the moss, crisscrossing the cord around the ball until the moss is securely wrapped around the root ball. Tie off the cord and trim the ends.

7

Cut two more cords slightly longer than the distance you'd like them to hang from the ceiling. Tie one cord to each side of the ball, tying them to the cord that is wrapped around the moss ball. Then tie the two cords together at the top, tying them together at the length at which you would like them to hang. Hang the ball and repeat the steps for the remaining two kokedama.

WATER

The amount you need to water will depend on the temperature, time of year, amount of light, and humidity. The best way to determine if your plants need water is to lift the moss and fern balls—they will be light-weight when they need water. In the warm, dry California summer, without air conditioning, I generally water every two days. Water the kokedama by either submerging the balls in a bowl, tub trug, or bucket of water or spraying them with a gentle shower. If you're dunking the balls, submerge the fern and moss ball until all the air bubbles have stopped coming up, soaking them for five to ten minutes. If you're using a hose or showerhead, soak the balls with water until they feel heavy with water. Let them drain in the shower, tub, or sink and then hang them back up. Mist daily to increase humidity.

LIGHT

Moss and ferns will do best in bright indirect light. They'll burn in direct sun.

MAINTENANCE

As with any living thing there will be a small amount of cleanup—bits of moss that fall on the floor or a dead fern frond from time to time. The twine will need to be replaced periodically.

Water Sculpture Garden

A simple but dynamic under-water sculpture garden.

By far the simplest project in this book, this display is some-what minimalist, but that allows the natural structure of the marimo to take on the appearance of an underwater sculp-ture. The marimo's velvet green color will enliven any space, and they work especially well for an area with low light. The small round stones add a contrast in size, and their dark color imparts a soothing waterscape. Put water in a jug the day before to allow the water to come to room temperature and chlorine to evaporate if you have chlorinated water.

Aegagropila linnaei, better known as marimo or moss balls, is a type of algae that grows into green balls in lakes in parts of the Northern Hemisphere. They make a great indoor water-garden plant due to their low-maintenance nature. They don't need any special care and can simply be kept in a bowl or vase.

A word of caution: don't be fooled by fake marimos. They are made of synthetic materials and look very smooth and are often sold in the decor section of pet or aquarium stores. Real marimo are available online or at your local aquarium store. If your local aquarium store does not have them, they can most likely order them for you—just ask.

MATERIALS

Small round river stones (A)

One rectangular vase (I used a vase that is 9 inches high × 7 inches wide × 4 inches deep) (B)

Three marimo balls (C)

1 Rinse the river stones and place them in the vase.

2 Add the room temperature water to the vase, to within a few inches of the top.

3 Gently place the marimo balls in the water, one ball at a time.

WATER

Change the water weekly—tap water is fine.

LIGHT

Too much light can harm the marimo balls. If your marimo balls turn white or begin to lighten in color they are receiving too much light. It is a good idea to roll the moss balls periodically in the water to change their position so that all sides of the marimo get enough light. You will know they are not getting enough light if they are turning brown and dying.

TEMPERATURE

Marimo are native to cooler water and prefer temperatures below 77°F. If you have placed your vase in a spot that heats up in summer, consider moving it to a cooler location, away from a window.

CLEANING

When you see dirt particles accumulating on the marimo you should clean them. A very dirty marimo will begin to brown. Gently squish it a few times in a container filled with clean water. You may then want to roll it in your hand a bit to prevent it from falling apart and to maintain its ball-like shape. If the ball does start to fall apart or turn black, the dark spots should be removed and the ball rolled into a ball again. Return it to the vase.

Saikei Tray Garden

Create a miniature world inspired by the Japanese art of tray gardening.

Making a tray garden is the perfect way to garden in the city. This miniature composition brings the serenity and calm of a natural landscape indoors. Saikei is a less formal style of bonsai, and combines living trees, rocks, and moss. This art form was developed in Japan by Toshio Kawamoto after World War II. Kawamoto wanted to make the art of tray gardening more accessible to gardeners by using less-developed trees, with an emphasis on the rocks and soil and overall appearance. In this saikei-inspired tray garden a young ficus bonsai is planted high up next to a large rock, with peat moss below and around the bonsai to hold the tree in place.

Many bonsai are intended for outdoor growing environments. For this project, select a species that can live as a houseplant. I used *Ficus benjamina*; other plants that can work long-term indoors and are good bonsai candidates are jade plant (*Crassula ovata*), *Punica granatum* (pomegranate), and *Sageretia theezans* (Fukien tea). If you use a seedling that has been growing outdoors but is suitable for indoor use you need to acclimate the tree by gradually moving it to an outdoor area with less and less sun over a two-week period. Indoor light, even in a bright area, is less intense than outdoors. *Ficus benjamina* does not like to be moved, so you may experience a complete leaf drop when you replant the tree. Don't be alarmed—it will recover and should have new leaf growth within two weeks.

MATERIALS

Live moss (A)

Peat moss (B)

Rectangular tray (I used a 6- × 12-inch ceramic platter) (C)

Small piece of bonsai wire (D)

2 pieces of plastic mesh (available at garden stores and online) (E)

Small-grain gravel (F)

Rock (I used a moss-covered 3½- × 5½-inch piece of granite) (G)

A bonsai start at least 3 years old that can grow indoors (H)

TOOLS

Bowl (I)

Drill (J)

Diamond hole saw bit ½ inch or ⅝ inch (K)

Needle-nose pliers with wire cutter (L)

Large tweezers (M)

If you have purchased live moss on the Internet, keep it moist until you are ready to plant. In a bowl, mix your peat moss with water until the peat moss is fully saturated but not sopping wet and allow it to sit for at least an hour.

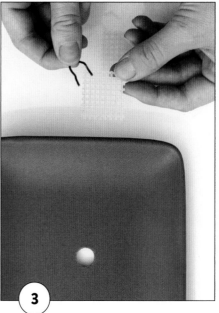

If you're using a tray that does not have a drainage hole, drill two drainage holes on the bottom. I drilled one about ¼ of the way in from each short end. Keep surface wet with water while you drill to prevent heat build-up and cracking.

Cut two pieces of wire to a length of an inch or less and bend them into a U-shape.

Cut two pieces of plastic mesh that are about 1- × 1-inch square. On the top side of the tray, place a piece of mesh over one of the drainage holes, hold it in place with one hand, and turn the tray over. Holding the plastic in place, insert one of the U-shaped wires into the hole and push it up through the mesh. Repeat with the other piece of mesh and the other U-shaped wire.

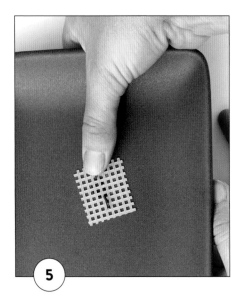

Bend the ends of the wires over the top of the mesh, about the same width apart as the drainage hole width, so that they hold the mesh pieces in place. If the ends are too long trim them. Be sure to make the hook of wire just barely fit into the drainage hole so that it holds the mesh tightly in place.

Place an even layer of gravel on the tray.

Place the rock on the tray, centered between the long sides of the tray. Leave enough room for the tree and soil on the right, and a few inches of empty space on the left. Align the center of the rock a little to the right side of the center of the tray, so there is room to put the tree next to the rock. The rock I used has a flat side that I have positioned toward the tree.

Take the tree out of the pot and determine which side of the tree you want to be the front. Place the tree to the side of the rock. Use as much peat moss as needed under the tree to make the tree level with the rock.

9

Pat more peat moss over the soil until you have a mounded shape that continues the slope of the rock.

10

Cover the peat moss with the live moss, pressing the live moss into the peat moss. Allow the moss to come to the edges of the right side of the tray. Leave the left side of the tray free of moss.

11

Use the tweezers to remove any bits of debris or dirt from the live moss and gravel. Level the gravel with the flat side of the tweezers.

WATER

Bonsai have little soil so watering frequently is key. In summer it may need to be watered as often as twice a day. To water, start at the edge of the moss and move inward. Water until the planting is saturated and water drains out of the drainage holes. Mist the moss at least once or twice a day. Humidity should be fairly high, which will be helped by the gravel on the tray. Placement in the kitchen or bathroom can also help if the other rooms in your home don't have very much humidity.

LIGHT

Both moss and ficus like bright indirect light. Place the planting near an east or west window in the fall, winter, or spring. In summer either filter the light with a sheer shade or move the planting away from windows.

MAINTENANCE

Remove vigorous new growth in spring and periodically throughout the growing season. Never remove all the new growth at one time—retain two or three leaves at the base of the shoot. Remove training wire (if any) after several months by snipping it into short lengths. Do not allow the wire to stay on the tree long enough to create scars.

Living Diorama

Make a shadow box come to life with living plants.

I have always loved dioramas. The joy of placing tiny logs and moss in a shoebox to create a simulated temperate rain forest in grade school has stuck with me. This project is a grown-up version of that miniature garden I created so many years ago. Taking cues from natural history dioramas, this living shadow box utilizes a mix of two-dimensional and three-dimensional objects. It is an opportunity to preserve the beauty and grandeur of a place you've visited or somewhere you might like to go. You can use any photograph you have as the backdrop for your scene. I used a lush tropical waterfall from a recent trip to Hawaii.

Have the photograph you want to use printed directly on metal by your local photo lab—it will remain unharmed if a stray drop of water or mist accidentally lands on it. I used basalt rocks and moss pressed into a bed of spray foam to continue the landscape from the two-dimensional to the three. The selaginella, placed in containers—which can be removed for watering—bring the piece to life. You could also use ferns, senecio, or rhipsalis—just keep in mind the feeling of the place in the photograph and try to continue in the same vein when selecting your plants. You want the plants to look like they belong with the photograph—as if they came out of the photograph.

The word *diorama* was coined by Louis Daguerre, a French photographer, in 1822. Daguerre created the original diorama in Paris, with help from a camera obscura, out of huge paintings depicting historical or picturesque scenes. Lighting would change the scene, simulating the passage

of time, a change in weather, or a sense of motion. Today our understanding of dioramas is thanks to full-size replicas or miniatures of a partially three-dimensional landscape. The diorama often displays a scene depicting a historical event, nature scene, or cityscape.

MATERIALS

11- × 14-inch metal photographic print (A)

11- × 14-inch shadow box, at least 2 inches deep (B)

Black basalt rock in small and medium pieces (C)

Four 2-inch selaginella plants (D)

11- × 14-inch black foam core (E)

Landscape black foam (F)

Four 2-inch coconut fiber pots (G)

Black silicone (H)

Dried green moss (I)

TOOLS

Utility knife (J)

Gloves (K)

1

Place the photograph in the shadow box and arrange the rocks and plants how you want them to appear in the diorama.

2

Using a utility knife, cut the foam core into a shape that mirrors the layout of your plants and rocks.

3

Wearing gloves and following the directions on the can, use spray foam to adhere the coconut fiber pots and rocks in place on the foam core. Hold the coconut fiber pots and larger rocks in place as you spray the foam around them.

4

Let the foam dry. Once it's dry cut off any excess foam. Place the foam core with the empty coconut fiber pots and rocks in the shadow box to make sure it fits. Cut off more foam if it does not fit.

5

To apply the silicone, work with the foam core in the shadow box or on a covered surface. Working in the shadow box will give you a better sense of the overall picture, but you will need to be careful when applying the silicone. (Working on a separate surface is safer, but you will have to imagine the photograph behind the foam.) Squeeze the silicone onto the coconut fiber pots and foam.

6

Immediately attach moss and small rocks to the silicone and let the silicone dry.

7

Keeping the selaginella in their original pots, place the plants in the coconut fiber pots. This makes it easy for you to water the plants—you can just remove them from the coconut fiber pots.

WATER
Remove the selaginella from the coconut fiber pots and water them in a sink or bowl. Selaginella is one of the few houseplants that love to stay damp—not dripping wet, but never dry. Try to keep the soil always moist. Mist the plants frequently; daily in a dry environment. If you get a little moisture on the metal print you don't have to worry about it getting ruined—it can handle the moisture. Misting helps provide the humidity that selaginella love.

LIGHT
Do not put the shadow box in direct sun—the foliage will burn. Bright indirect sun is ideal.

FERTILIZER
Feed a maximum of once a month spring through fall with a balanced liquid fertilizer diluted by half.

PROPAGATION
Selaginella is easy to start from cuttings. Take stem-tip cuttings in spring or summer. Place the cutting in soil and keep moist until they've rooted.

Wardian Case Terrarium

An ode to the original terrarium, this glass house is full of life and color.

The Victorian Age brought with it an explosion in gardening. The romantic vision of nature blossomed as more people lived in urban environments, isolated from the natural world. In the late 1820s an English doctor named Nathaniel Ward came upon the idea for a miniature version of the large glasshouses that were then popular. His miniature glasshouse, a precursor of today's terrarium, was called a Wardian case. Suddenly there was a way for the avid botanists of the time to safely transport exotic plants home from around the globe.

There are two types of terrariums: open and closed. Closed terrariums are covered and have high humidity. For a closed terrarium, choose plants that love humidity and that will do well in bright indirect light (closed terrariums should not be placed in direct sun; they get too hot). Open terrariums can tolerate a little bit of sunlight, but not too much, as the glass can act as a magnifying glass and burn the plants. For an open terrarium, choose plants that like more sunlight, like cacti and succulents. When you're deciding which type of terrarium to use, consider the light conditions in your home.

African violets, discovered in 1892, are the perfect plant for a closed terrarium, because they thrive in humidity. In their native habitat, the Usambara Mountains of East Africa, African violets enjoy 70 to 80 percent humidity. Other great plants you could use in this closed terrarium are hypoestes or pilea, or a fern.

I used insect specimens to represent the live hatching butterfly that many original closed terrariums housed. Eventually the butterfly and beetle specimens will decompose in the humid air of the terrarium. To slow this process I've coated the insects with a clear spray paint. It may not protect them completely, but it will slow the absorption of moisture and prevent mold, giving them more durability in the humid conditions of the terrarium. Do not let the bugs come into direct contact with the moss—it will create mold on the insects. In this project I've mounted the butterfly on a small piece of wood so that it doesn't touch the moss, and I've positioned the beetle on a pin half an inch up from the moss.

MATERIALS

Wardian case with a removable top and hatch for ventilation and a plastic tray at the bottom of the case (A)

Crushed gravel (B)

Chipped charcoal (C)

Sheet moss (D)

Potting soil (E)

4-inch African violet (Saintpaulia ionantha**)** (F)

Haircap moss (G)

Cushion moss (H)

1 or 2 pieces of found wood, about 3 to 4 inches long with a 1-inch diameter (I)

2 to 3 mounting pins

3 insect specimens (J)

Scrap paper

Clear spray paint (use a glossy one for the beetles) (K)

1

Take the top off the Wardian case.

2

Pour a 1-inch layer of crushed gravel into the tray.

3

Cover the gravel with a thin layer of charcoal, which will filter the water and reduce odor.

4

Press the sheet moss over the charcoal—it will function as a barrier between the soil and drainage material.

Layer the potting soil on top of the sheet moss.

About one third of the way in from the left side pull the sheet moss back to make a hole for the African violet in its pot.

Place the African violet, still in its pot, into the depression. (I leave the African violet in the plastic pot for three reasons: African violets tend to not bloom if they're overpotted—they tend to bloom better if they're pot-bound. A general rule of thumb is that the pot should be one-third the size of the span of the plant. Also, I like to be able to water the African violet separately from the moss. And last, if the plant gets more light from one side I like to be able to rotate the plant so that its exposure to light and potential growth is equal.)

Place the haircap moss around the African violet's pot so that the pot is no longer visible. Push the moss down so that it makes contact with the soil.

On the other side of the terrarium place the cushion moss, using more in some places to give the topography some variety by making smaller and larger mounds.

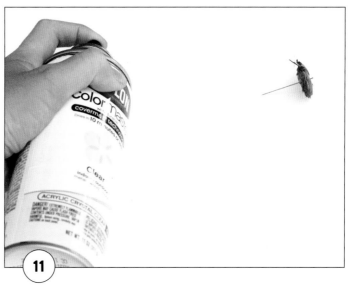

Position the pieces of wood in the gravel on the right-hand side, so they stand just short of vertical.

Push a mounting pin through a beetle specimen and place the beetle on a piece of paper. Spray the insect with the clear spray paint, being careful to cover the whole specimen, especially its bottom side. Let the spray paint dry and repeat. I did not spray my butterfly because of the delicate nature of its wings. I've had it in a terrarium for a year and it is still in perfect shape. Repeat with the other insect specimens.

Once the insects are completely dry, place them in the terrarium. Pin them securely to the wood or moss. If you mount them on the moss be sure to leave a half-inch gap between the beetles and moss to help prevent deterioration from mold.

WATER

A closed terrarium retains moisture and recycles the water for a long period of time. You want to have some moisture in the terrarium, but not so much that there is a buildup of moisture. A closed system needs very little water. If you see water droplets building up on the inside of the glass you have overwatered. If the terrarium walls have more than 25 percent condensation, remove the cover until the walls clear. You may have to do this more than once. In a closed terrarium, there should be only occasional clouding. If you begin to get any rot or mold you have overwatered and will need to replace those plants and insects. The presence of mold or mildew indicates that one of three things is wrong: the terrarium may contain too much water, air circulation is poor, or you are using plants that do not do well in closed terrariums. Remove infected plants immediately and correct the environment by letting the terrarium dry out or by increasing its air circulation. The moss will go through an acclimation phase, during which it may need more water than normal. It should establish itself within a few months. Once the moss has adjusted to its new home spritz it with a sprayer two to three times a week. (How often you'll need to spritz it will vary depending on your location, temperature, and how often the lid is open.)

Water the African violet separately with a watering can that has a narrow spout using lukewarm or warm water. You will know it needs water when the soil is dry. You can use

your finger to feel if the soil is moist. The best way to water is to remove the African violet from the terrarium and place it in a saucer. If using a watering can or faucet to water from the top, avoid getting water on the leaves. Let the African violet sit in the saucer with the water for a half an hour to an hour. Once the plant has absorbed all the water it needs return it to the terrarium and discard the excess water. African violets should be allowed to dry out between waterings.

LIGHT

Closed terrariums should not be placed in direct sun, as the temperature inside will get so hot the plants will melt. African violets and moss do well with bright indirect light. They do well near a window, but out of direct sunlight. Watch out for cold wintertime night temperatures—if it is a cold night, take the terrarium away from the window and only return it once the morning sun has warmed the space.

MAINTENANCE

Remove the cover of the terrarium for a few hours every week, or open the vent to provide some air circulation. Pinch off any old blooms and their stems to encourage new growth. If you notice any mold or rot clean it out immediately so that it doesn't spread, and try to get the terrarium back to an optimal level of humidity and moisture. Keep it away from vents, radiators, air conditioners, and fans to avoid drafts and sudden temperature changes. You may need to periodically clean the glass, for your benefit and the plant's, because dirty glass can diffuse the amount of light the plant is receiving. If you develop any pests or insects cut out infected areas and spray with insecticide.